Educating Children with AD/HD

A Teacher's Manual

PAUL COOPER
and
FINTAN J. O'REGAN

ROUTLEDGE / FALMER
Taylor & Francis Group

London and New York

First published 2001
by RoutledgeFalmer
11 New Fetter Lane, London EC4P 4EE

Simultaneously published in the USA and Canada
by RoutledgeFalmer
29 West 35th Street, New York, NY 10001

RoutledgeFalmer is an imprint of the Taylor & Francis Group

© 2001 Paul Cooper and Fintan J. O'Regan

Typeset in Sabon by Keystroke, Jacaranda Lodge, Wolverhampton
Printed and bound in Great Britain by TJ International Ltd,
Padstow, Cornwall

British Library Cataloguing in Publication Data
A catalogue record for this book is available from the British Library

Library of Congress Cataloging in Publication Data
Cooper, Paul, 1955–
Educating children with AD/HD : a teacher's manual / Paul Cooper
and Fintan J. O'Regan.
p. cm.
Includes bibliographical references and index.
1. Attention-deficit-disordered children–Education–Handbooks, manuals, etc.
2. Attention-deficit-disordered youth–Education–Handbooks, manuals, etc.
3. Attention-deficit hyperactivity disorder—Handbooks, manuals, etc.
I. O'Regan, Fintan J. (Fintan Joseph), 1960– II. Title.
LC4713.2 .C66 2001
371.93–dc21   00–069680

ISBN 0–415–21387–8

Educating Children
with AD/HD

Attention Deficit/Hyperactivity Disorder (AD/HD) is the most common behavioural disorder affecting up to 5 per cent of children in the UK. This book provides a concise and comprehensive guide to educating children with AD/HD. It offers a theoretical introduction to AD/HD and practical guidance to the classroom teacher on how to support children with this condition.

The book is divided into three sections:

- Part One focuses on the nature of AD/HD and its impact on the individual in school, as well as the ways in which it can be most accurately diagnosed
- Part Two addresses the principles and practices of intervention, including specific educational interventions and behaviour management techniques
- Part Three is structured around a series of case studies illustrating the nature of AD/HD and its relation to other difficulties, and makes suggestions for school-based interventions

The book is rooted in the experience of practitioners who work on a daily basis with children with AD/HD, and draws upon up-to-date research evidence on the topic. The authors challenge crude assumptions about AD/HD and argue that the best way to understand AD/HD is as a condition in which biological and environmental factors interact.

The book is suitable for use as a teaching manual and a training resource. It will help teachers, other educational workers and students develop a sense of empowerment in relation to AD/HD.

Paul Cooper is Professor of Education at the University of Leicester. He is also a chartered Psychologist and former school teacher. He has authored and co-authored many books on educational matters, including *Emotional and Behavioural Difficulties: Theory to Practice* (with Smith and Upton, Routledge: 1994) and *Positive Alternatives to Exclusion* (with Drummond, Hart, Lovey and McLaughlin, RoutledgeFalmer: 2000).

Fintan J. O'Regan is Headmaster of the Centre Academy in London, which is recognised as the first established school and evaluation centre in the UK for the diagnosis, teaching and management of students with AD/HD.

Contents

Acknowledgements

To Mack R. Hicks for his vision in laying the foundations for the teaching and management of AD/HD children in the UK and to Susie Lee for her continued love and support on behalf of the cause.

Part 1:
Understanding AD/HD

This opening part of the book deals with the nature of AD/HD in terms of its origins, and the biological, psychological and social influences on its development.

1
AD/HD
What it is, and what it isn't

Main topics:

- AD/HD defined
- Pseudo AD/HD

AD/HD DEFINED

The term Attention Deficit/Hyperactivity Disorder originates from the fourth edition of the Diagnostic and Statistical Manual of the American Psychiatric Association (APA, 1994). This is the most recent version of the diagnosis which has gone through many changes since a biologically based problem of inattentiveness and overactivity was first proposed by the English paediatrician George Still in 1902 (Still, 1902). It should be noted that there is a similar diagnostic criterion published by the World Health Organisation (1990) referring to a condition known as 'Hyperkinetic Disorder' (HD). Although there are important technical differences between the two criteria, from the teacher's viewpoint the two diagnoses can be treated as identical. This book will refer throughout to the American version of the diagnosis since, at the time of writing, it is the one that teachers are most likely to encounter. (See Appendix 1 for a note on similarities and differences between the two diagnostic criteria.)

Key Features of AD/HD

Key features of the AD/HD diagnosis are *inattention*, *hyperactivity* and *impulsivity*. These can be defined more fully in terms of children who display some of the following behavioural characteristics, based on the APA diagnostic criteria (APA, 1994).

Inattention

- often fails to give close attention to details or makes careless mistakes in school-work, work, or other activities
- often has difficulty sustaining attention to tasks or play activities
- is easily distracted from tasks and play activities
- often does not seem to listen when spoken to directly
- often does not follow through on instructions and fails to finish schoolwork, jobs, or duties in the workplace (not due to oppositional behaviour or failure to understand instructions)
- often has difficulty organising tasks and activities
- often avoids, dislikes or is reluctant to engage in tasks that require sustained mental effort (such as schoolwork or homework)
- often loses things necessary for tasks or activities (e.g. toys, schoolwork, pencils, books or tools)
- is often forgetful in daily activities

Hyperactivity/Impulsivity (1) Hyperactivity

- often fidgets with hands or feet or squirms in seat
- leaves seat in classroom or in other situations in which remaining seated is expected
- often runs about or climbs excessively in situations in which it is inappropriate (in adolescents and adults this aspect may be limited to subjective feelings of restlessness)
- often has difficulty in playing or engaging in leisure activities quietly
- is often 'on the go' or often acts as if driven by a motor
- often talks excessively

(2) Impulsivity

- often blurts out answers before questions have been completed
- often has difficulty awaiting turn
- often interrupts or intrudes on others (e.g. butts into conversations or games)

Sub-Types

There are three main ways in which AD/HD manifests itself:

1. The mainly hyperactive sub-type
2. The mainly inattentive sub-type
3. The combined sub-type (both hyperactive and inattentive)

This highlights the fact that not all people with AD/HD are overactive or behaviourally disruptive. Individuals with the mainly inattentive form of AD/HD, far from being intrusive, are often easily ignored and neglected.

<u>Caution:</u>

simply behaving

in some or even all of these ways

does not mean

that a person has AD/HD

For the AD/HD diagnosis to be made, the diagnosing clinician (usually a paediatrician or child psychiatrist) must be satisfied that the following conditions have been met:

- the number and type of symptoms should be consistent with the conditions laid down in the diagnostic criteria, meaning that the child must display *six or more* of the symptoms from the inattention list, or *six or more* from the hyperactivity/ impulsivity lists

- the problems must have persisted for at least *six months* to a degree that is *maladaptive* and *inconsistent with the child's developmental level*

- there must be evidence that some of these symptoms were present *before the age of 7 years*

- problems are *pervasive* across two or more settings, e.g. at school (or work) and at home

- there must be clear evidence of *clinically significant impairment in social, academic or occupational functioning* (i.e. the symptoms must interfere *significantly* with the individual's emotional, educational, or professional functioning)

- the symptoms are not directly related to a Pervasive Developmental Disorder, Schizophrenia or other Psychotic Disorder, and are not better accounted for by another mental disorder (as described the DSM IV, e.g. Mood Disorder, Anxiety Disorder, Dissociative Disorder or a Personality Disorder).

PSEUDO AD/HD: WHAT LOOKS LIKE AD/HD, BUT ISN'T AD/HD?

Clearly, every one of us at some times displays some or all of these characteristics. In most mainstream school classrooms, most children will at some time be inattentive, impulsive or overactive. A few children will have all of these behaviours in their repertoires. Most people when they are tired, bored or under pressure will not be able to concentrate as well as they usually can and may be easily distracted. Some people, when they are excited, bored or anxious may act impulsively, become fidgety or restless. Children may display some or all of these behaviours when they are physically ill or otherwise stressed, for example, as a result of personal problems, family trauma or because they are anxious or disturbed by something.

If the behaviours of concern can be directly associated with external stressors, then before the possibility of AD/HD is considered efforts must be made to remove these stressors, or, where appropriate, help the affected individual to learn effective ways of dealing with the stressors. If the behavioural difficulties are directly the result of external problems then it is unlikely that one is dealing with a case of AD/HD, but rather that one is confronted with Pseudo AD/HD (Hallowell and Ratey, 1995). The characterisitics of Pseudo AD/HD are that it:

- looks like AD/HD
- is temporary/episodic
- is directly associated with situational factors
- is not pervasive.

Obviously, pseudo AD/HD is likely to be a lot more common than genuine AD/HD.

HOW MANY PEOPLE HAVE AD/HD?

Estimates of the incidence of AD/HD vary, worldwide, between 1% and 6% of the school-age population (Tannock, 1998). In the USA the most commonly agreed estimate is that AD/HD affects:

- 3–5% of all Americans
- 5–7% of school-aged children.

In the United Kingdom it has been estimated that:

- 1.8% of children experience Hyperkinetic Syndrome (i.e. severe hyperactivity), and that this is a sub-group of the (approximately) 5% of school-aged children who have AD/HD.
- If we estimate average class size in state schools in the UK at thirty students, then this means that, on average, there will be between one and two children in *every class* with AD/HD. Of course the distribution will not be even, with some schools and classes having a disproportionate number of students with AD/HD. A recent study, for example, found that 70% of students in a special school for youngsters with Emotional and Behavioural Difficulties (EBD) qualified for the AD/HD diagnosis (Place, *et al.*, 2000).
- Boys outnumber girls 4:1 in the hyperactive/impulsive/mixed type groups, as they do for most acting-out behavioural problems.
- Boys and girls are represented in about equal numbers in the non-hyperactive (mainly inattentive) group.

These points should help to dispel the misguided idea that the AD/HD diagnosis can be applied to any 'naughty' child. Such indiscriminate use of the concept is clearly wrong. Neither is it correct to apply the AD/HD label to all children who might otherwise be termed to be experiencing 'emotional and behavioural difficulties' (EBD), which is estimated to comprise between 10% and 20% of the school-age population of England and Wales (Young Minds, 1999). Having said this, these figures indicate that the problem affects a substantial minority of all school students, and a very substantial poportion of those deemed to experience emotional and behavioural difficulties. As such AD/HD is likely to be encountered by the majority of teachers at some time in their career.

2
AD/HD in the Classroom:
Teacher and Student Perspectives

Main topics:

- Common Classroom Problems
- What it feels like to have AD/HD

COMMON CLASSROOM PROBLEMS ASSOCIATED WITH AD/HD

In the classroom the child with AD/HD is likely to display some or all of the following problems in most settings, and to a degree that is seriously disruptive to their own and/or others engagement in the learning process (based on Taylor, 1994):

- Being frequently out of seat at inappropriate times and in inappropriate situations
- Deviating from what the rest of the class is supposed to be doing
- Not following the teacher's or other supervising adult's instructions
- Talking out of turn or calling out
- Being aggressive towards classmates
- Having a short attention span and being very easily distracted
- Bothering classmates, hindering them in their work efforts, or preventing them from concentrating
- Being oblivious and daydreaming
- Losing and forgetting equipment
- Not handing in homework or handing it in late
- Producing work that is incomplete or sloppy

By and large schools are places where student conformity and passivity are assets to the smooth running of things. On this basis it could be said that AD/HD is tailor made to disrupt schools as we know them. It could also be said with equal truth that schools are tailor made to exploit the weaknesses of students with AD/HD. In short, we must be careful not to assume that problems relating to AD/HD are necessarily located within the student. The doggedness with which the majority of school students quietly put up with sometimes pointless, tedious and stressful school routines is often under-emphasised. There are not many legally compulsory institutions, apart from schools (and possibly prisons), where human beings are routinely subjected to strict rules regarding their rights of association and communication, physical movement and personal appearance, and where failure to comply with rules can lead to punishment. In these circumstances it is sometimes the case that the child with AD/HD is telling us more about what is wrong with the school than what is wrong with the child.

Children with AD/HD are often experienced by parents, teachers and peers as puzzling and frustrating

This is because the problematic behaviour associated with AD/HD often combines with evidence of more positive behaviour. For example, it is commonly reported (e.g. Barkley, 1990, 1997) that in one to one situations with adults, in highly novel situations, or, sometimes, for no obvious reason, children with AD/HD will perform tasks in ways that indicate that they do not have difficulties with inattentiveness, impulsivity or hyperactivity. This can create the impression that the child's apparent inability to sustain attention or control motor activity or impulses at other times is the result of laziness or lack of motivation. This interpretation misses the point that *a central problem for children with AD/HD is sustaining an even level of performance in school work and other tasks and activities.* Sensory stimuli, such as incidental sights and sounds which most children will experience as only minor distractions are experienced by the child with AD/HD as highly intrusive. This will mean that others may sometimes be unaware of the distractions which interfere with the concentration of the child with AD/HD. Again, this will sometimes lead people to accuse the child with AD/HD of wilful disobedience or plain laziness, when in fact it is more a problem of *hypersensitivity* (Barkley, 1997). A typical interaction between the child with AD/HD and the adults in their life will often take the following form:

> *Adult*:   Why can't you behave like other children?
> *Child with AD/HD*:   I don't know why . . .

The problem is that the adult assumes that the child has control over factors that the child experiences as being beyond their control.

WHAT IT FEELS LIKE TO HAVE AD/HD

For the individual who has AD/HD the core problems of inattentiveness, impulsiveness and/or hyperactivity are major sources of difficulty. But this is only part of the personal experience of AD/HD. In addition to the core problems the child with AD/HD experiences a bewildering array of difficulties which arise from the process

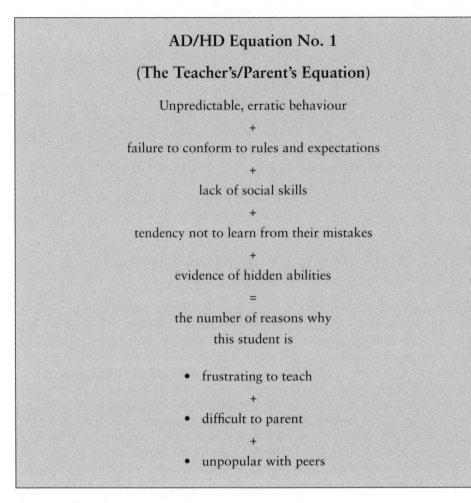

Box 2.1

of interacting with other people. Some of these problems derive directly from the core problems of AD/HD, others are associated with their experience of other people's reactions. The difficulties include:

- I'm always getting into trouble at home and at school because I do things wrong, or I do the wrong thing or I don't finish things.
- My parents and teachers are disappointed in me.
- People are unfair: even though I try very hard people seem always to complain that I am lazy.
- I don't see things in the way that other people see them.
- I just don't seem to understand how other people think and feel.
- I feel like an alien.
- People sometimes think I'm odd.
- People often ignore me or don't like me.

- Sometimes people laugh at me.
- I have difficulty getting on with other people.
- Sometimes I get very miserable because of these problems, and sometimes this makes me angry.
- I just wish people would leave me alone.
- I'm always forgetting things.
- I am no good at school work.
- I am useless at just about everything.

AD/HD Equation No. 2

(The student's equation)

All the times I try, but get things wrong

×

all the times I am blamed for not trying when I am trying

=

the number of reasons why I feel rejected, useless

+

fearful of taking the risk of trying again

Box 2.2

The following are longer quotations from students diagnosed with AD/HD attending a special school (from Cooper and Shea, 1999), describing their experience of various aspects of AD/HD. As you will see, different students react in different ways to the experience of AD/HD, reminding us that it is often a mistake to make simplistic assumptions about AD/HD or students with AD/HD.

On AD/HD and School Routines

Put it this way: a person with ADD – someone with AD/HD or ADD would not last five minutes in my [old] school. Because they wouldn't know when to go to classes. In my old school it was all very timed – down to the last second – always timed. For instance, a lot of people would look at their watches and when their watch said – whenever the time was to stop – they would get up and leave! OK? And that's how it would all work! They all get up at once and leave! There was lots of times when the teacher just stopped talking and said: 'That's it!' And then you'd get up and leave. But there was never any bells and buzzers in our school.

(Christian, 16)

On Being Disruptive

I don't think I had any control, because when I got into a temper I could try and talk not loud, but then I thought, 'Ughhhh!' And I would get all stressed out.

Sometimes at home I would like – I wouldn't mean it – but sometimes I would just like shout. You know, like I would think people were shouting, but they're not. And when I was talking, it would sound like I was talking really loud. And sometimes I wouldn't notice I was talking really loud. My mum would say: 'You're shouting!' And I would say, 'No I'm not!'

(James, 15)

Sometimes at the end of school it would be quite difficult, 'cause like they would have homework out on the board. Then they would say to me an' Daniel, 'Write it out!' And it would take us quite a while to write the thing out. And we never used to do any homework. I used to say, 'I can't do this!' And then he [the teacher] used to go: 'Well you go and write it out now!' And in the end I just didn't do it. If I can't learn at school, how am I supposed to do homework? You know!

(Daniel, 14)

Well [at first] I was always good at home, and at school. When I got up to first grade things started to change. I was kind of good in school. And I built up a lot of steam at school and I would take it out at home – like on my mom, my sister or my dad. Mostly my mom or my sister. And in the end it started to change. I would be good at home, and I would take my steam out at school. That's when I started getting into fights and stuff.

I have a bad temper. If someone starts me off and they go a little too far, I have a go at them.

(Ian, 14)

On Being Impulsive

Sometimes I can't help saying what I feel!

(Herbert, 13)

I never think before I do something. Sometimes [it] happens – if I'm like thinking: 'If I do this, I'm going to get into trouble.' But I never normally do that. I'll do it, and until afterwards, it's OK. So I do something bad and afterwards I realise that I've done something bad, and that I shouldn't have done it.

(Jeff, 12)

I used to be mad! I just used to do stupid things. I used to fight a lot and stuff. Being rude to teachers and all that. Doing stupid things like trying to jump off ten foot walls and stuff. That sort of thing. Ugh! I remember I went on the train tracks once! Things like that! The trains were running at the time.

They weren't actually there at the time. It's sort of electric as well. And the trains go about 70 miles an hour. Someone threw my skateboard on the railway tracks and that's why I went over.

(Joe, 14)

One time when I was living in a bungalow, and we had a fire in the fireplace, [I remember] taking the hot ashes out of the fireplace and [I] put them in the garage on paper. Two minutes later: fire!

I remember my mother telling me [that] I was trying to play horsey on Homer's [a pet dog] back, and I ripped out two big bundles of fur. And he turned round, and he snapped at me, right here [just below one eye]. I ripped out bundles of his fur. It was an accident – he didn't mean to hurt me, 'cause he was really a lovely dog.

(Joan, 13)

On Concentration Problems

[. . .] when my mum asks me to do stuff, like say empty the dishwasher. And then I would get distracted or something. And I wouldn't do the dishwasher, because I would forget about it. And then she would come and yell at me because I didn't do it.

(Hope, 13)

I've always had a problem with concentration and attention. [. . .] Well, sometimes in class, I wouldn't be able to concentrate. And I'd be talking to other people. And I wouldn't be concentrating on my work. And part of that was because I was at a young age. And I've matured a lot since then. I've actually got much much better. In the last year and a half. But there's always that little concentration thing, of me not being able to concentrate. And me not being able to settle down and get on with a piece of work. Which I feel is a drawback.

(Christian, 16)

I've had a hard time starting that [essay on *The Merchant of Venice*]. And it's not because I don't want to do it; it's because I find it hard to concentrate on it.

(James, 15)

They found that I had difficulties paying attention in my old school. I always used to talk to my friend. I used to never pay attention. Some of my friends are hyper; some have difficulty in reading and spelling. But I don't have those. I have difficulty with paying attention.

(Kate, 12)

I'm always the type of person who struggles, 'cause that's just me.

(Janine, 13)

On the Diagnosis

> *Ian*: It just means that I don't pay attention in class, and when things get boring, I just block the teacher out and just ignore 'em, [then] I get in trouble. It makes learning hard.
> *Interviewer*: At school?
> *Ian*: Yeah.
> *Interviewer*: How about in other places?
> *Ian*: As long as it's fun and hands on – like watching my dad build things. Like he's an excellent engineer. He's excellent with cars. And I've seen him do things one time, and I can do the exact same thing. I love doing things like that.
>
> (Ian, 13)

> I don't like it. Well I don't like having it. Well, I was born with it. Well most of the time people are born with it, or something evolves in their blood, or something. I don't know. Most of the time people are born with it. I think it's just passed from generation to generation. I don't know. I thought that I just lost a couple of screws in the head.
>
> (Janine, 13)

> *Interviewer*: What does ADD mean for you?
> *Janine*: That I have a problem with me that really I cannot solve myself. Sometimes, when I was little, I thought that I was an alien; that I was different from others. Because if I walked down the street everyone's normal and I'm like an alien really; going down the street and everyone's like, really weird.
> *Interviewer*: What made you think that, do you think?
> *Janine*: I don't know, because I thought that I was different from the others, and I didn't really care about me because – well like, I cared about me – but I didn't care about me much, because I just thought that I was really different. And that I wasn't the type of person I should be.

> [the diagnosis provides] the meaning of why I was having difficulties.
>
> (Kate, 12)

> Well, I realised that whenever I got into trouble at school for talking and stuff, it wasn't my fault; it was because I had ADD. I couldn't help being distracted and that I wasn't concentrating properly.
>
> (Hope)

> [I] tell people [I've got AD/HD] if they ask me what's wrong with me, and if they tell me I'm mad [I say] 'I'm not mad. I've just got something wrong with me.' It just makes me a bit active sometimes.
>
> (James)

On Medication

Interviewer: Was it important to you to find out about AD/HD at all?
Kate: Well, not the diagnosis, just the Ritalin. Finding out that I had to take it helped me.
Interviewer: So do you think it was important to find out why you had trouble concentrating in [previous school]
Kate: I don't think it was important. I just think that it was the reason that I was doing it.

When I'm on it [Ritalin] I work harder, and I'm nicer, but when I'm out of school [and not on Ritalin] I'm sometimes silly, or I act stupid, or do things that I wouldn't really do if I was on the Ritalin. [. . .]
  [When I'm on Ritalin] I have more control over what I say [. . .]

(Kate)

When I'm taking Ritalin I'm calmer. I can study more and everything. And when I'm not I really can't concentrate or anything.

(Stacy, 13)

I can concentrate better on Ritalin, I think like. I get on with my work more, and I don't talk so much.

(James)

It makes me – Ritalin and Pemoline things – they make me think first. I can think for myself anyway, but they make me think even better for myself.

(Joe)

Sometimes I like it [Ritalin], but sometimes I don't. [. . .] If I do take it when we didn't have school, I wouldn't want to go outside and play with my friends, or, I would just want to stay home by myself and read a book or watch television or something.
  [. . .] if I'm on Ritalin, I find it easier to do the work. Or if I don't find it easier I just go up to the teacher for help. And we had to do a report on *The Woman in Black* – the book that we just read – and he helped me on it just a bit. And I was on Ritalin, and I did the whole report by myself, and I didn't ask for anyone's help. And I got an A plus on it, so.

(Leslie, 14)

I like being myself instead of like calm, and everything like that.

(Janine)

Joan: Well, I'm just being the way I am, and people want me to change. They want me to calm down more. But I do calm down.
Interviewer: Do you think that you need to calm down?
Joan: Yes. But I still want to be – I still want to have fun.
Interviewer: So, when you calm down, do you feel like you have less fun?

Joan: Yes.

Interviewer: Can you tell me about it: where people have wanted you to calm down?

Joan: Like in the Chinese restaurant. Like if I've had my pills, I don't enjoy – if I've had my pills it makes me too sleepy, and I don't – I do enjoy my food, but I don't eat very much.

[The pills] calm me down, to help me work. They help me calm down, so I don't embarrass my mother.

If I didn't have my tablets my mother wouldn't be able to handle me the way that she does.

I just don't want to take Ritalin anymore. In my opinion, I never thought that it helped very much. It did help a little bit, but I never thought that it did that much for me. I only take it because if I don't take it they'll chuck me out.

I would probably take it before an exam.

(Christian, 16)

Interviewer: Do you take tablets?

Herbert: What, Ritalin?

Interviewer: Yeah.

Herbert: No.

TS: Did you ever?

Herbert: No. And I never will either. They muck up my head!

Interviewer: So, they muck up your head. That would be the bad side. Do you know why people take them? Is there a good side?

Herbert: To calm them down and concentrate on their work. Umm. I don't need that!

Interviewer: Do you think you need help concentrating on your work?

Herbert: No. I can concentrate. As long as there's not a lot of noise. If people can shut up and stop talking, yeah, easy, I can concentrate. But if there's a lot of noise, I won't concentrate. Simple as that. The teachers can't keep the class under control. They don't keep me under control, do they? Simple as that!

(Herbert, 15)

The Experience of AD/HD: Joseph's story

This is 24-year-old Joseph's account of what it feels like to have had AD/HD throughout his school career and beyond:

'It seems that every time I have tried to explain the problem of AD/HD and its manifestation people have responded with a dismissive comment like: "Ah sure we all get that." I have, therefore, given up bothering to even try to explain the condition. I know this is a defeatist reaction but I also know that I just don't have the emotional energy or stamina to carry on banging my head against a brick wall. Basically, when people say "We all get that", what they really mean is: "You're a hypochondriac! Stop making excuses and blaming others for the way your life is turning out!" Indeed I don't feel too optimistic about the plight of any AD/HD sufferer trying to convince anyone but the most educated or supportive professional or friend.

'I remember as a child attending a country school by where my parents lived. The principal there saw me as some kind of evil distraction cast upon him by the devil. Indeed I used to think that the devil was in him because of the hard time he gave me. Not that I was completely undeserving of this. I was the bane of any classroom: wild, impulsive, easily distracted, attention seeking, very emotional and generally highly volatile. For me, learning certain subjects was virtually impossible. Although I did often think myself to be thick, I was never fully convinced of this, as there was, I felt, something bright about me.'

(Abridged from Cooper and Bilton, 1999)

Box 2.3

3
AD/HD and Other Problems

Main topics:

- AD/HD and Emotional and Behavioural Difficulties (EBD)
- Assessing AD/HD
- AD/HD and other problems: behavioural, emotional and educational

AD/HD AND EMOTIONAL AND BEHAVIOURAL DIFFICULTIES (EBD)

Emotional and Behavioural Difficulties (EBD) is the term commonly used by British educators to describe a wide range of individual, social and personal difficulties which manifest themselves in behaviour which is disruptive to the individual's social and educational development, as well as, in some cases, being disruptive to the teaching and learning processes for others. As we noted in Chapter 1, current estimates place the population of children believed to experience EBD at between 10% and 20% of all school age children (Young Minds, 1999). EBD does not describe a single 'condition', but is rather an umbrella term for a wide range of difficulties. AD/HD is one such difficulty that can be seen as a sub-category of EBD. Having said this, current evidence suggests that AD/HD is present in high proportions among populations that might qualify for the label of EBD. A recent study found that 70% of students attending an EBD special school qualified for the diagnosis (Place *et al.*, 2000), other studies of school-age children and young people have found that AD/HD co-occurs with other clinically defined disruptive behaviour disorders, such as Conduct Disorder and Oppositonal Defiance Disorder (Pliszka *et al.*, 1999) in between, approximately 50–60% of cases, with some studies finding rates as high as 80% (ibid). One British study found that 100% of children with Conduct Disorder also qualified for the AD/HD diagnosis (McArdle *et al.*, 1995) (see section below on AD/HD and co-occurring conditions). Other features of AD/HD indicate that it is:

- a life-long condition for between 50% and 70% of people diagnosed with it

- believed to have a biological basis, in that it is caused in part by dysfunctions in the brain's neurotransmission system which impair the operations of the frontal lobes that are the seat of powers of impulse control and self-regulation

- often treated with stimulant medication

- associated with situational problems that might arise from the stress and strain of trying to cope with a child with genuine AD/HD.

ASSESSING AD/HD

For any diagnosis of AD/HD to be reliable it should be based on rigorous and extensive assessment procedures (see Detweiller *et al.*, 1999). Assessment should involve the gathering of data on the child's functioning in different circumstances, and from a wide range of sources.

Qualitative assessment (i.e. concerned with people's perceptions and beliefs) can include gathering information, in the form of interviews and/or questionnaires, from:

- the child

- family members

- peers

- teachers.

Quantitative assessment of the child's functioning in psychological, medical and educational terms can be gathered through the application of:

- standardised tests of cognitive performance, administered in self-completed questionnaires and formal interview

- computerised tests of vigilance and attention

- medical examination (including tests of hearing and vision).

AD/HD AND OTHER PROBLEMS – BEHAVIOURAL, EMOTIONAL AND EDUCATIONAL

AD/HD commonly co-occurs with a wide range of other behavioural, emotional and learning problems. These additional (or 'co-morbid') problems relate to the core features of AD/HD in different ways, with some being a direct result of the core problems and others being the results of social and interpersonal factors surrounding AD/HD. That is, they can sometimes be the result, in part at least, of the ways in which others react to the child's AD/HD symptoms. There follows a brief survey of some of the major overlapping conditions. (The percentages are approximations based on averages from various sources).

Overlaps Between AD/HD and Other Behavioural Problems

- 50–60% of children with AD/HD display oppositional and defiant behaviour, often losing temper, arguing with adults, refusing to comply, deliberately annoying others.

- 45% of children with AD/HD display conduct disorder, in the form of chronic aggression towards others, destructive behaviour, deceitfulness or theft, serious and chronic rule breaking.

- 25% of children with AD/HD display antisocial or delinquent (i.e. criminal) behaviour.

Overlaps Between AD/HD and Emotional Problems

- 30% of children with AD/HD display clinically defined anxiety disorders.

- 33% of children with AD/HD experience major clinical depression.

- 50%+ children with AD/HD display emotional problems.

- 50%+ children with AD/HD show severe social skills problems.

Overlaps Between AD/HD and Learning Problems

- 90% of children with AD/HD are under-productive in school work.

- 90% of children with AD/HD underachieve in school.

- 20% of children with AD/HD have reading difficulties.

- 60% of children with AD/HD have serious handwriting difficulties.

- 30% of children with AD/HD drop out of school in the USA.

- 5% of people with AD/HD complete a 4-year degree course in a college or university in the USA, compared with approximately 25% of the general population.

4
Biology, Brains and AD/HD

Main topics:

- AD/HD and the brain I: the psychology of AD/HD

- AD/HD and the brain II: the biology of AD/HD

- AD/HD and families: genetics and AD/HD

AD/HD AND THE BRAIN I: THE PSYCHOLOGY OF AD/HD

Cognitive research on individuals with AD/HD has produced a number of theories about the precise nature of the psychological impairment involved in AD/HD. Most of these theories tend to agree on the view that, of the three core features of AD/HD (attentional problems, impulsiveness and hyperactivity), the overriding problem is that of impulse control. It is not the case that children with AD/HD do not *want* to conform to rules and behave in orderly, organised and co-operative ways. Neither is it the case, necessarily, that they do not *know* what the desirable form of behaviour is in a given situation (though this should never be taken for granted). Rather, the problem resides in the psychological (cognitive) mechanism of self-regulation. This means that the psychological machinery that we all rely on to stop ourselves from doing things that are not in our best interests can be said to be malfunctioning for the person with AD/HD. In psychological terms people with AD/HD are characterised as experiencing significantly greater problems than most in inhibiting or delaying a behavioural response.

Impulse Control is the Key

Tony and Liam both know that if they don't hand in their Maths homework on Monday they will get a detention. But it's Friday, last lesson. It's been a long hot, sunny week. The classroom is stifling. Teacher and students would all rather be somewhere else. After 60 agonising minutes the bell finally rings. As always the homework is on the whiteboard. Mrs Fowler, a genial and popular teacher, says, 'If you haven't copied it down already, as soon as you have copied down the homework, you may go.' Both Tony and Liam are restless and desperate to leave. However, before the echo of the teacher's last word has faded Liam is on his way home, without having copied the homework down. Tony stays to copy down the words from the whiteboard, because he knows (as does Liam), that if he doesn't do the homework he will have a detention and still have to do the homework. The difference between them here is that Tony considers the consequences of not writing down the homework and responding to his impulse to leave, whilst for Liam the impulse to leave is overwhelming. Although he knows the likely consequences of this behaviour, this knowledge is not drawn on at the right moment, and used to make a decision. In fact a decision-making process has not taken place, in Liam's case, he has simply reacted without reflection. On the way home, during a moment of calm, he suddenly remembers about the homework, and resolves to phone Tony to get it from him. Then he is distracted by an item in a shop window. The next time he thinks about the homework is when he is being asked by Mrs Fowler to hand it over. . . .

Box 4.1

Filtering Our Urges: The Importance of Executive Functions

The American clinician and researcher, Russell Barkley (1997), presents a cognitive model of AD/HD which is based on the hypothesis that physical characteristics of the brains of individuals with AD/HD lead to problems with *executive functions*.

Executive functions are mental processes which human beings employ to make decisions about how to behave. They act as the filter through which our sudden urges to do things pass and are checked. Imagine you are driving to an important appointment. You are late. You are distressed and anxious. You are frustrated by the slowness of the traffic. A great deal depends on this meeting. To be late will be very bad for you. You are stuck behind a slow-moving lorry. What stops you from giving in to your urge to do something rash, like overtake the lorry when it stops at a red traffic light? The answer to this question is that you engage in processes of reflection and appraisal which in turn lead you to make a decision about whether or not to act on your urge.

Executive functions involve:

* *Working Memory*: described as a 'mental workbench' (Baddeley, 1986) on which bits of information are held and made available for the operations of other executive functions.

- *Internalised Speech*: the process of inner dialogue whereby, for example, we weigh up/compare and contrast bits of information held in working memory.

- *Motivational Appraisal*: involves taking account of our own motivational state.

- *Reconstitution, or Behavioural Synthesis*: recalling knowledge of similar situtions to the current one.

In the case of our example, these executive functions will, most often, lead us through a sequence of reasoning, which will go something like:

> I am anxious and frustrated at the delay. However, if I overtake this lorry and go through a red traffic light there is a risk that I could cause an accident, and injure and kill myself and other people. Being late for this, or any other, meeting is much less important than other people's and my own safety. If I were to cause an accident I would be prosecuted, and would never forgive myself if I caused serious injury to another person. Therefore, I will not overtake this lorry unless it is absolutely safe so to do.

In practice the internal dialogue is unlikely to be as clear and formal as this. For most of us this appraisal process would be hard to articulate, because it will be composed of a mixture of verbal, visual, auditory and other forms of reflected experience. However, it is likely that all of us engage to some degree in a version of these processes when confronted with a situation such as the one we are considering, though in practice we probably experience the process as an instantaneous event: we contemplate the dangerous manoeuvre but put a stop to it immediately, perhaps because an image springs to mind of an accident scene, or we recall a memory of a friend or relative being injured, or we are suddenly aware of the possible legal consequences of our actions.

The problem with executive functions, and working memory in particular, is that they have a limited capacity. We can only hold on to so much information at a time, and the efficiency of these functions can be affected by other factors, such as stress or anxiety. So if we accept Barkley's hypothesis that problems with executive function lie at the heart of AD/HD then it follows that not only will individuals with AD/HD experience more difficulty than most in managing their impulses, they will have even greater difficulty when placed in stressful situations, such as when under social or emotional pressure.

This last point is supported by the Dutch researchers Sergeant (1995), Van der Meere (1996), and Borger and Van der Meere (2000). Their research shows that individuals with AD/HD are capable of what might be termed 'normal' levels of sustained effort and concentration in certain carefully structured and controlled situations, and where the task is stimulating. This research shows that a major feature distinguishing individuals with AD/HD from those without AD/HD is the ability to return to the concentration task after being distracted from it.

Both of these theories have important implications for the education of children with AD/HD, as will be shown in later chapters. For the present it is sufficient to note that whilst there is strong evidence to suggest that AD/HD is underpinned by particular cognitive characteristics, the extent to which these characteristics are seen to be problematic is influenced by circumstances, i.e. *the condition of AD/HD is strongly affected by situational factors*.

AD/HD AND THE BRAIN II: THE BIOLOGY OF AD/HD

Brain imaging research has found abnormalities in the frontal lobes of the brains of individuals with AD/HD, where the systems responsible for regulating attention are located. Other studies have found particularly low levels of activity in certain neurotransmitters which are responsible for making connections between different areas of the brain.

The causes of these abnormalities are various:

1. In approximately 70% of cases the dysfuntion is inherited.

2. Between 20% and 30% of such brain dysfunction is caused by one of the following environmental factors:

    • brain disease: such as encephalitis

    • brain injury: as a result of physical trauma to the head

    • toxin exposure: as a result of alcohol or drug abuse; exposure to lead during the pre- and peri-natal stages of a child's development.

It is important to note that AD/HD can be mild, moderate or severe, and that the moderate and mild forms may not always have a significant physiological component.

AD/HD AND FAMILIES: GENETICS AND AD/HD

There is strong evidence from studies carried out over the past thirty years that AD/HD is more common in the biological relatives of children with AD/HD than it is in the biological relatives of children who do not have AD/HD (Tannock, 1998). Twin studies have repeatedly shown a much greater incidence of AD/HD among identical (monozygotic) twins than among non-identical (dizygotic) twins. Similarly, studies which compare the incidence of AD/HD among children and parents who are biologically related with that of children and parents where the child is adopted, have shown that there is a much greater chance of AD/HD appearing in parents and children when they are biologicaly related (ibid.).

These findings are given further weight by molecular genetic research which has identified certain genes as being implicated in the presence of AD/HD and AD/HD type symptoms. In particular there is evidence that genes in the dopamine system are implicated in AD/HD (ibid.). Dopamine is a neurotransmitter (see above) which is found in systems of the brain concerned with, among other things, the regulation of movement (Thompson, 1993).

5
AD/HD and Destiny

Main topics:

- What happens to people with AD/HD?
- AD/HD and the bio-psycho-social approach

WHAT HAPPENS TO PEOPLE WITH AD/HD?

As we noted earlier, AD/HD is for many people a lifelong condition. If not dealt with effectively, AD/HD can put individuals at high risk of such diverse problems as:

- social isolation
- relationship problems
- difficulties in obtaining and sustaining employment
- criminality
- motor accidents
- psychological problems, such as depression.

People with AD/HD are often seen as:

- incompetent
- disorganised
- aggressive

- lazy
- disruptive
- untrustworthy
- neglectful
- selfish
- accident prone
- antisocial or asocial.

Children with AD/HD are more likely than most to:

- fail in school academically, in spite of the fact that they tend to score in the average to above average range on standardised ability tests (Hinshaw, 1994; Barkley, 1990)

- be excluded from school (in the UK) for behavioural reasons (Hayden, 1997).

Adults with a history of AD/HD (or AD/HD type symptoms) are at greater risk than most of experiencing marital breakdown (Hinshaw, 1994) and imprisonment (Farrington, 1990).

Having said this, there are widely (even wildly) varying estimates claiming that between 30% and 70% of children and juveniles diagnosed with AD/HD 'grow out' of the condition (Hinshaw, 1994). Some of the variation in these statistics can be accounted for by the fact that AD/HD was for many years considered a childhood disorder, with the result that affected adults tended to be diagnosed with alternative 'adult' disorders, such as depression.

AD/HD AND THE BIO-PSYCHO-SOCIAL APPROACH: AD/HD IS A PRODUCT OF NATURE *AND* NURTURE

The consensus among researchers who have investigated AD/HD is that the condition is underpinned by biological factors (see above). This is not the same as saying that AD/HD is wholly caused by biological factors, or that an individual possessing the biological traits associated with AD/HD will automatically develop AD/HD. As we have noted, there is evidence to suggest that a substantial proportion of individuals who have AD/HD as children cease to have it in adulthood. Furthermore, the negative outcomes associated with AD/HD, such as social, emotional, behavioural and learning problems, can be reversed through effective educational, psychological (Hinshaw *et al.*, 1998), and pharmacological (Greenhill, 1998) interventions. So how do we make sense of the relationship between biological and other individual, social and environmental factors in the creation of AD/HD?

Disorder versus Difference

First we need to distinguish between the idea of 'disorder' and that of a 'difference'. The biological features of AD/HD certainly suggest that the brains of people with

AD/HD are different, in a range of respects, from those of the majority of the population. The evidence would also suggest that these brain differences lead to certain specific cognitive differences, in the form of the ease with which individuals are able to inhibit their response to a behavioural stimulus. The extent to which this cognitive characteristic is a problem (i.e. a 'disorder') depends on certain factors, in particular: the external situation and the individual's adaptive and compensatory skills.

There are situations where it is advantageous to act with minimum reflection, such as in escaping a dangerous situation, in a game requiring speedy reactions, or immediate improvisation. Of course, where the situation demands a more reflective, steady and sequential approach this characteristic is going to be of less value and may even become a problem. Having said this the individual may limit the extent of the problem by exercising adaptive or compensatory skills. For example, individuals may manage their impulsiveness by employing routines for regularly monitoring their behaviour, and using self-prompting techniques to ensure that they think before acting on impulses. In this way AD/HD is no different from many other individual differences in which biological factors are implicated. Individuals with hearing impairments can learn to lip-read, a child with a mild visual impairment can partly compensate for this by sitting closer to the whiteboard or OHP screen. Furthermore, the effective teacher will support students to minimise the extent to which their individual differences act as a barrier to learning. This is done by making adjustments to the learning environment, helping the child to develop compensatory skills, and finding opportunities for encouraging individuals to exercise their strengths and talents. We will deal with educational interventions in detail later in the book.

The point is that a disorder, such as AD/HD, is inevitably a product of the interaction between individual characteristics and life experience. By the same token, the life experience can do a great deal not only to prevent the development of a disorder, but to make assets out of individual differences. Sportspersons and actors are often praised for their 'energy' and the 'instinctual' qualities of their performances, when the same behaviours in other settings might be condemned as hyperactive, 'over the top behaviour', or 'impulsive'. Similarly, what is 'undisciplined' or 'illogical' thinking in one context, might be seen as 'creative' and 'lateral' thinking in another. Consider the difference between a car repair manual and a poem, or a road map and an abstract painting: the first of each pair require very different qualities from the second, though both are valued.

The pattern of interaction between biology and experience (or 'nature' and 'nurture') is illustrated in simplified form in Box 5.1. The central implication of this model is that the behaviours seen by the teacher, parent or peers of the child with AD/HD are influenced by a range of factors in addition to the child's biology, in particular: the child's experience of the world (e.g. has it been generally nurturing/ affirming or negative/aversive?); their maturational level (physical / cognitive / social / emotional); the quality of their compensatory skills (e.g. self-management strategies); their level of motivation to overcome difficulties.

Having said that there is no biological reason alone why individuals with the particular neurological and cognitive characteristics associated with AD/HD should develop the disorder, we have to acknowledge that in practice the circumstances which young people commonly experience, especially in school settings, are increasingly aversive to children with the kinds of cognitive characteristics associated with AD/HD. This point can be illustrated through reference to some of the findings of research into home-based education. It is argued that home-based education tends to be a more

---

Interaction between Biology and Experience

Biological Differences
(e.g. genetic; disease)

LEAD TO

Brain Differences
(e.g. physical structure of frontal lobes;
neurotransmitter system)

LEAD TO

Cognitive Differences
(e.g. problems with executive function)

LEAD TO

Core Problems
(e.g. impulsiveness; attentional difficulties; hyperactivity)

Mediating Factors:

Experience   Maturation

Compensation   Motivation

LEAD TO

Behavioural Manifestations
(i.e. the behaviour we see)

Based on Frith (1992)

Box 5.1

successful option than school-based education for many children because of the ability of families to be far more flexible in meeting the learning needs of children.

Meighan (2000) cites a range of issues which illustrate the strengths of home-based education and common weaknesses of school-based education. Below, we reflect on these and their implications for children with AD/HD. Our intention is not to suggest that children with AD/HD should be educated at home, but rather to use the debate about this topic to highlight ways in which the educational needs of children with AD/HD are shared by the vast majority of children in school.

• *Natural learning and 'dovetailing'* describe processes of learning through interaction that is often a natural part of the early learning experience shared by child and carers. Central to this approach is the need to seize incidental opportunities to capitalise on the child's immediate interests and to 'dovetail' sophisticated learning experiences into a child's existing behaviour.

School curricula which are tightly prescribed, time-limited, test-oriented and objectives-led make this kind of approach to learning difficult in schools. Children with the cognitive characteristics associated with AD/HD find it difficult to adjust to such a prescriptive regime, though they will benefit from opportunities to pursue their own interests.

• *Different forms of discipline* are necessary for different situations. 'Discipline' is used here in its widest sense, to refer to the regulation of behaviour and thinking. Effective and flexible learning will require the ability to work under the authority and direction of others, co-operatively with others, and autonomously, as the situation demands.

Individuals with AD/HD can learn the skills of obedience, co-operation and self-regulation. It is so often the case, however, that before they get the chance to learn, they fall foul of authoritarian forms of school discipline and are further punished for failing to be co-operative and self-directing when they have not had the opportunity to learn these skills.

• *Variations in learning style* can be easily catered for in the home or small group environment. Unfortunately our schools, partly as a result of the narrow focus of the curriculum, tend to overemphasise the value of reflective and analytical learning styles, sometimes to the exclusion of others. This causes particular problems for students with the cognitive characterisitcs associated with AD/HD, who often favour physical and activity based approaches to learning over reflective approaches.

• *Different types of curriculum* are appropriate for different purposes. The traditional 'imposed subjects' type, which dominates mainstream schools, lends itself to situations where a body of knowledge needs to be transmitted. Where the intention is to develop students' research and self-instructional skills it is useful to employ some form of negotiated curriculum, in which the student has a major say in defining aims and content. The child with the cognitive characteristics associated with AD/HD will benefit from a varied approach to the curriculum because it will capitalise on his or her strengths for individualism whilst also giving him or her access to established knowledge forms.

• *A non-hostile learning environment* is essential to the learning needs of all students. Unfortunately, the widespread phenomenon of bullying, the constant preoccupation of schools with issues of disruptive behaviour, and the high levels of permanent and temporary exclusions indicate that schools can often be highly aversive environments. This is particularly the case for students who are the victims of bullying, who are disaffected, disruptive and/or the victims of the disruptive behaviour of others, or who are at risk of exclusion. Students with the cognitive characteristics associated with AD/HD are at risk of being in all of these categories.

Of course, the advocates of home-based schooling rightly assert that all children are likely to benefit from the positive circumstances they describe, and to be impeded in their learning by the negative circumstances they identify. The point we wish to make is that *students with the cognitive characteristics associated with AD/HD are more vulnerable than most to the common negative influences of mainstream and other educational settings*, and are among the least well equipped to tolerate or otherwise 'put up' with such aversive circumstances. In fact it is a principle underpinning this book that mainstream and other educational settings will benefit all their students if they take on approaches which set out to meet the specific needs of children with the characteristics associated with AD/HD.

Evidence of the Relationship between Experience and AD/HD

There has been research which has identified patterns of parental behaviour that have been related directly to childhood AD/HD. For example, Barkley (1990) in a review of research on this topic refers to studies which show that children with AD/HD tend to experience a high level of interpersonal conflict with their parents. Furthermore, the mothers of children with AD/HD have been found to be more commanding and negative in their behaviour towards their children than the parents of children who do not have AD/HD. Barkley cites further evidence which shows that children with AD/HD tend to experience more commanding and negative behaviour from adults and children from outside the family (such as teachers and peers), and that when the children's AD/HD symptoms subside, (e.g. when the child is placed on medication) the mothers' levels of disapproval and frequency of commands decreases. He concludes from this that it is the child's AD/HD which precedes the parents' negative behaviour rather than the other way around. This is the basis for the important claim that bad parenting or ineffective teaching do not in themselves *cause* AD/HD. What does seem to be the case, however, is that the kinds of interactions that children with AD/HD experience do have an effect on the way in which their AD/HD manifests itself, and in some cases the extent to which it is seriously or not so seriously debilitating or disruptive.

Recently published research by Nigg and Hinshaw (1998) which examines the relationship between parents' personality traits and childhood AD/HD provides interesting findings which may bring us closer to an understanding of the way in which the biological, psychological and social factors interact. Principally, their carefully designed study found an association between specific parental characteristics and the nature and manifestations of children's problems. Children with AD/HD were found to be more likely to have a mother with marked anxiety symptoms or one who had experienced a recent major depressive episode than children not diagnosed with AD/HD. Children who exhibited AD/HD co-occurring with Conduct Disorder and Oppositional Defiant Disorder had fathers who scored lower on measures of 'agreeableness' and higher on measures of 'neuroticism' than fathers in the comparison group. Thus, this study indicates that the extent to which a child with AD/HD exhibits seriously anti-social behaviour is influenced by the characteristics of parents.

Clearly, the evidence just presented might be interpreted through a bio-medical/ genetic model and it be suggested that the children inherit anti-social characteristics from their parents. This suggestion, however, has to be put alongside the well-established research tradition which places considerable emphasis on psycho-social factors as being chiefly implicated in the aetiology of anxiety disorders, with some, though at present limited, evidence of inheritability (Mills, 1996). Where Oppositional Defiant Disorder is concerned, Blau (1996) reports that environmental explanations are the most persuasive. Common to both Oppositional Defiant Disorder and Anxiety Disorders is the implication that problems with the parent-child bonding process are significant factors in creating difficulties, causing affected children to find themselves trapped at the stage of infant dependency, sometimes into their adolescence and beyond.

Part 2:
Principles and Practices for Intervention with AD/HD

In this section we look at some of the basic principles and practices related to effective intervention for children with AD/HD, with an emphasis on the multi-modal approach.

6
The Multi-Modal
Approach to Intervention

Main topics:

- Educational, medical and other professionals working together
- The role of medical intervention
- The contribution of school staff to a multi-modal approach
- Establishing a whole school approach
- Partnership with child and parents
- Evaluating progress

EDUCATIONAL, MEDICAL AND OTHER
PROFESSIONALS WORKING TOGETHER

As we have already shown, AD/HD is a multi-faceted problem comprising a complex array of interacting biological, psychological and social factors. In the opening chapters we have focused mainly on the educational aspects of AD/HD; however, it should be remembered that, to qualify for the AD/HD diagnosis, the core symptoms must be demonstrated to the extent that they are causing severe problems in at least two settings, usually the school and the home. It is not surprising, therefore, that the child with AD/HD, in addition to having problems at school, often experiences serious problems in the home situation. Often, there is an interaction between home and school problems, with problems in one setting exacerbating problems in the other. For example, school and parents may come into conflict over the student's behaviour, with each side blaming the other and refusing to accept any share of the responsibility for doing anything about it. Another, sometimes related, scenario involves the student carrying the frustration and stress from one setting into the other, so that frustration and anger that have built up at school are released in the form of tantrum behaviour in the home situation. Not surprisingly, these conflicts in turn can come to be associated with secondary emotional and behavioural problems.

For these reasons it is often necessary to take a multi-modal approach (Barkley, 1990) to intervention with AD/HD, of which the educational input is one, albeit central, part. Other professional members of the intervention team might include some or even all of the following:

- General Medical Practioners
- Health Visitor
- School Nurses and Medical Officers
- Paediatricians (including school doctors)
- Child Psychiatric Services
- LEA Behaviour Support Service
- Educational Psychologist
- Social Services
- Educational Welfare Officers
- Other Specialist Services (Special Educational Needs Services and Provision; Speech and Language Service)

While these different workers each have their own specialist role to play, it is important that there is good communication between all the professionals involved and that steps are taken to ensure that they are working in a concerted and coherent way, and that they are consistent in their approaches and practices. A failure to secure such co-operation can leave vulnerable and fragile clients confused and even more distressed.

In some areas it may be difficult for education professionals to be accepted, or to establish clear lines of communication with other professional groups. This will probably be the case where there is no history of multi-disciplinary working, or where experience of this has been unsuccessful. In these circumstances school personnel need to be proactive in developing such links. This can be achieved through making direct contact with other professionals, and will be facilitated if this is done with the support of the student's carer(s).

THE ROLE OF MEDICAL INTERVENTION

It is easy for AD/HD to be viewed solely as a medical problem, and for it to be dealt with as such – that is, as an issue centrally concerning the patient, his/her carers and a medical doctor. Undoubtedly, there are important medical aspects to AD/HD, and at the current time the concept is contained within a medical framework and in the form of a medical diagnosis. The problem with a medical diagnosis, in our view, is that it tends to exaggerate the individual aspects of the problem, by placing the emphasis on changing (i.e. 'treating') the individual, rather than looking at the individual in his or her wider social (including educational) context, which, as we have already noted, requires considerable attention.

It should be pointed out, however, that medical approaches do not only lead to the prescription of medication, there are some physicians who adopt other approaches, including dietary interventions (Kinder 1999), and 'alternative' or 'holistic' forms of medicine. In some parts of Japan the preferred intervention for AD/HD is a form of physical therapy known as Dohsa Hou. The Dohsa method, which was first developed by Gosaku Naruse (1975) is a 'holistic' approach to therapy (Harizuka, 1998) based on an appreciation of the interactive relationship between bodily movement and internal psychological processes. The approach is used with a wide range of disorders in addition to AD/HD, including cerebral palsy, autistic spectrum disorders, schizophrenia and severe learning difficulties.

Although there is an increasing demand for approaches to dealing with AD/HD which go beyond, or simply avoid, the use of medication, it has to be recognised that, at the time of writing, medication is widely used by physicians in the treatment of AD/HD. In the USA over 90% of children with AD/HD are receiving medication of some type (Greenhill, 1998). In the UK the proportion is much lower with one estimate suggesting that only 10% of children with AD/HD are being medicated (Munden and Arcelus, 1999). The National Institute of Clinical Excellence (NICE, 2000) puts the proportion of children with AD/HD receiving methylphenidate (Ritalin) at less than 6%. It is important to stress that it is widely agreed by informed clinicians that whilst medication is sometimes a necessary part of treatment, it is *never*, in itself, a sufficient treatment (Hinshaw, 1994). The role of medication, such as methylphenidate, is to facilitate the learning of appropriate behaviour and skills by placing the child in a situation whereby their receptiveness is maximised (see Kewley, 1999). Thus, in the case of methylphenidate, the child's ability to concentrate is improved. This creates *a window of opportunity* through which parents and teachers can begin to help the child develop strategies and habits for effective learning and self-regulation. It is important to note that there is research evidence to suggest that whilst medication of this type is often successful in alleviating the symptoms of AD/HD (Greenhill, 1998), other forms of non-medical intervention, such as behavioural interventions, have been found to intensify the positive effects of medication, and in some cases lead to reductions in dosage (Hinshaw *et al.*, 1998). This multi-modal approach is endorsed in the UK by the government's National Institute for Clinical Excellence, as well as the British Psychological Society (BPS, 2000).

THE CONTRIBUTION OF SCHOOL STAFF TO A MULTI-MODAL APPROACH TO AD/HD

School personnel play a vital role in the assessment of and intervention with AD/HD, at all phases of education. Teachers, particularly at the pre-secondary stages, are often second only to primary carers in terms of their level of knowledge of and contact with a child. School personnel may independently suspect that a child is suffering from AD/HD, or do so in concert with carers. Either way, the relationship between the carers, the school staff and the child is of central importance. This relationship needs to be positive and characterised by a shared commitment to meeting the needs of the child through a co-operative approach. Every school should have ready access to an educational professional who is conversant with the concept AD/HD, be able to identify aspects of the school setting which may exacerbate the child's difficulties, and be prepared to make appropriate changes and accommodations where necessary.

Where assessment is concerned, school staff will play a vital role, in some respects mirroring that of the parents, by providing detailed information about the child's current and previously observed educational and behavioural functioning.

At the intervention stage the knowledge that school personnel have of circumstances in which the child functions effectively may be even more valuable than knowledge of his or her difficulties, as a basis for selecting intervention strategies. If the child has a statutory statement of special educational need relating to the problems of AD/HD then this may be a source of further support for the total intervention package. Where medication is prescribed school personnel will play a key role in monitoring its effects. This will enable the prescribing doctor to adjust the dosage if necessary. Similarly, school staff will be important sources of information about changes in the child's behaviour in school over time, and thus indicate either the effectiveness of intervention or that a new assessment or evaluation of the child's circumstances be undertaken.

The school can also be a site where the child can begin to learn more about the nature of AD/HD, and how to overcome its potentially debilitating consequences. Included in this process will be structured opportunities to learn appropriate ways of interacting with peers.

ESTABLISHING A WHOLE SCHOOL APPROACH

It is commonplace nowadays to talk about the need for whole school policies for everything. With regards to AD/HD it is neither necessary, nor even desirable, to have a policy devoted solely to AD/HD. After all, if we have a separate policy for AD/HD, then why not a separate policy for autism, Asperger's syndrome, dyslexia, asthma, athlete's foot, and so on. What is important is that core school policies are informed by a recognition of the fact that students have a wide range of needs and differences, and the nature of these differences should be taken into account when policies are being developed.

An understanding of AD/HD can contribute to the development of whole school policies in a number of ways. It is important to note that many of the measures which are essential for students with AD/HD are also likely to be of significant benefit to all students. We would go as far as to argue that any school which scrutinises itself from the perspective of the student with AD/HD will go a long way towards finding out what is required to improve the quality of the school experience for all students and other members of the school community.

Transparent Structures and Routines

It is essential that all structures and routines be streamlined, straightforward and clear. This applies to such things as the way in which the school day is structured. All members of the school community will benefit from an unambiguous, practical and uniform school timetable, free of idiosyncracies and exceptions. This means that areas where confusion might occur must be identified and addressed. For example, bizarre as it may seem, there have been schools where the precise time when the school day begins is a source of confusion, with some staff requiring students to adhere to one time, and other staff requiring the same students to adhere to a different time! Having the daily routine represented pictorially and displayed prominently helps to clarify and reinforce it.

Teaching and Rewarding Pro-Social Behaviour

It is often said that students with AD/HD do not have a problem with knowing how to behave, but rather they have a problem behaving in accordance with what they know (e.g. Goldstein, 1995). Because people do not tend to go through the mental mediation processes described above (i.e. in relation to executive functions) they are not making use of what they do know about how they should behave. Having said this, it is always dangerous to assume that students necessarily know how to behave. One of the consequences of the social rejection and/or neglect often experienced by people with AD/HD is that they do not get the same opportunities as most other people to learn and practise social skills. After all, how does a child learn how to behave at a children's party if s/he is never invited to one? This means that the teaching and positive reinforcement of pro-social behaviour should be consciously undertaken by staff in schools. Such skills as turn-taking in conversations and active listening, as well as the more 'heavyweight' skills of conflict resolution should be taught to all children, ideally through role play and discussion. In turn, when these skills are demonstrated in real-life situations they should be acknowledged and reinforced through praise.

One of the best ways of supporting and reinforcing the teaching of pro-social behaviour to students is through staff modelling the desired behaviours in their day-to-day interactions with colleagues and students alike.

Bullying Policy

An obvious indicator of the quality of a school environment is the way in which bullying is dealt with. It is inevitable in any organisation that from time to time incidences of bullying will occur in which people exploit the vulnerabilities of other individuals to exert power over them in a threatening way. Students with AD/HD can be on either side of the bully–victim divide, and in some cases may occupy both roles at once. In any event, they, and the rest of the school community, will benefit from a policy which stresses the need for honesty and openness around issues of bullying.

There are numerous existing approaches to bullying that might be called on to inform a school-wide bullying policy. Two commonly used approaches are the 'no-blame' approach and the 'bullying court' (Sullivan 2000).

The *no blame* approach stresses the need for the bully to be encouraged to empathise with the victim, and to explore what it is like to be on the receiving end of bullying. It is argued that if we blame the bully we tend to reinforce the bully's need to defend him/herself, which can easily turn into an offensive response, thus reinforcing the bully's sense of oppositionality. Instead of blaming the bully, the no-blame approach seeks to forge an alliance between bully and victim, the object of which is to help the bully see things in a new and positive way.

The *bullying court*, on the other hand, sets out to change the bully's behaviour by exposing it publicly by requiring that bullies face their victims and have their bullying behaviour subjected to open scrutiny and the judgement of their peers.

Each of these approaches has its merits and will be suited to different settings. The bullying court, for example, is a powerful way of raising the profile of bullying, of reinforcing existing rules relating to bullying, and of using the bullying issue in the context of citizenship education. At the same time, the greatest strength of the no-blame approach is that it requires the bully to explore and take ownership of his or her own behaviour and its effects.

In identifying an approach to the problem of bullying (and any other problem for that matter) it is important to remember that students with AD/HD will tend to respond better in calm, low-pressure situations, where there is a minimum of distraction, and where there is a very clear focus for attention and activity. This would tend to favour the no-blame approach. On the other hand, students with AD/HD will respond to powerful and clear-cut behavioural consequences, which favours the bullying court approach. This would suggest that a combination of these approaches would be the best route for most schools to take, combined, of course, as we have already noted, with the need for an emphasis on positive social behaviour, as well as a clear rule structure.

Unambiguous Rules

It is universally recognised that effective behaviour management policies are always underpinned by a small number of very basic rules (Walker, Colvin and Ramsey, 1995; Laslett and Smith, 1995). It is usually suggested that there should be between four and six basic rules for the whole school, which are designed to regulate individual and social conduct throughout the school, particularly in the public areas of corridors and playgrounds. They may also relate to the treatment of physical property, both personal and school, and also to issues of school dress. The intention of this set of rules is to summarise in a memorable way the general social ethos of the school.

In order that the rules be both memorable and practical they should be (1) expressed briefly in terms easily understood by the pupils, and (2) framed, where possible, in positive terms (i.e. stating what students should do, rather than what they should not do). One way of ensuring that the first condition is fulfilled is to involve the students in formulating the rules. This will also encourage student ownership of them. The second condition can sometimes be more difficult to achieve. The value of a positive rule is that it provides a reminder about what to do, as opposed to simply saying what one should not do. Such rules will act as a useful prompt for all students, but will be indispensible for the student with AD/HD.

It is also appropriate sometimes for there to be rules for specific contexts, such as classrooms in subject departments where particular conditions prevail (e.g. science labs, workshops, gymnasia, modern languages classrooms). Again the same principles apply: rules should be few in number, expressed in positive terms, and be in students' own language.

In both cases the rules should be posted prominently, and ideally with pictorial illustrations. The more attractive and interesting the mode of presentation, the more they are likely to be scrutinised by students, and, thus, remembered. Furthermore, one of the characteristics sometimes associated with AD/HD is a preference for pictorial as opposed to written presentation. The process of devising pictorial representations of rules can be passed over to students, and this again will help to make the rules accessible to students and thus engender a sense of ownership. It should be remembered that tasks such as this will not only play to the strengths of students who have skills in drawing and graphic design, it will also provide opportunities for students who are creative thinkers to conceptualise possible scenarios for others to realise pictorially. Although we should be cautious about over-stressing the link between creativity and AD/HD, it is the case that children with AD/HD, because of the difficulties they commonly have with literacy skills, may have their abilities to think in creative and divergent ways overlooked (see Crammond, 1994).

Breaks and Lunchtimes

It is well known that in most schools lunchtimes and breaktimes are likely to be sites where behavioural problems are most likely to occur. As we have already noted, students with AD/HD benefit from having clear structures and routines. In many schools, breaktimes and lunchtimes are periods when disruptive behaviour is likely to occur more often than it does in other more structured periods.

Obviously, the playground and other leisure areas should be subject to social and behavioural rules like anywhere else in the school. As always the rules should be few in number, phrased positively, expressed in students' language, and displayed graphically in a prominent place. Rules of conduct, however, in both playgrounds and classrooms, will be most effective when they provide the background for carefully structured and engaging student activities. These activities have to be planned, resourced and supervised just like teaching sessions. This is not to say that the playground should be a place where students are not free to pursue their own interests and to relax and socialise with each other. On the contrary, these activities should be available to all. What has to be acknowledged, however, is the enormous difference between relaxation and mind-numbing boredom. Opportunities to engage in organised and supervised games, clubs or individual activities (e.g. computer games) for short periods will help make breaktimes stimulating and purposeful. The engagement with others in structured, co-operative play will also contribute to the development of social skills.

'Recess Deprivation'

One thing that experienced teachers know all too well is that when children are deprived of the opportunity to get out of the classroom and 'let off steam' in the playground their behaviour and concentration levels deteriorate. This perception is supported by research findings that showed a direct relationship between levels of recess (i.e. playtime) deprivation and increases in disruptive behaviour and in-attentiveness (Pellegrini and Horvat, 1995; Pellegrini, Huberty and Jones, 1996). In several studies, it was shown that students of wide-ranging abilities could maintain high levels of concentration on classwork and minimal levels of disruptive behaviour for significant periods of time, provided the task was well planned, stimulating and age-appropriate. Even when these vital conditions prevailed, however, there was a time limit beyond which concentration levels and behaviour inevitably deteriorated. Once this time limit was reached the students entered the zone of 'recess deprivation' that could only be remedied by students being given access to breaktime activities (see previous section). After a brief activity break, students in these studies were able to return to classwork and to resume the former high levels of concentration and positive behaviour, until the same time limit was reached again. The implications of this are clear: teachers will get the best out of children if classwork is well planned, stimulating and interspersed with frequent short periods of physical activity. In Pellegrini *et al.*'s studies of middle school children the average time limit was about 40 minutes. The period of physical activity does not have to be long: perhaps no more than ten minutes in an hour. This means that in order to take advantage of this insight into recess deprivation it is not necessarily the case that children need to be given more breaktime, but that the existing time needs to be dispersed more evenly throughout the day.

Meeting Personal Needs: Being Safe, Cared for and Valued

As we noted in Chapters 2 and 3, a wide range of other social, emotional and behavioural problems often accompanies AD/HD. All of these problems have important consequences for students' relationships with others (both inside and outside school) and their inner selves. For all students, and for children with difficulties like these in particular, it is important to have a sense of being valued at a personal level within the school as a whole. One way of thinking about this is in terms of each student needing to feel safe, cared for and seen by others as having a valuable contribution to make to the school community (Cooper, 1993).

Safety needs are met when students feel that the school is an orderly place, and when they are secure in the knowledge that the school is being run fairly, on the basis of a transparent set of principles and rules. Such feelings of security can contribute to students' sense of being cared for. This in turn depends on the quality of human relationships within the school. The way in which staff generally relate to students sets the model that students will follow. Crucial qualities here are those of civility and personal respect. Rule structures and disciplinary regimes that are overly rigid can be experienced as impersonal and inhumane, thus provoking disaffection. This is why they are most successful when they are tempered by humanistic principles which enable rules and procedures to be applied intelligently, and where necessary with flexibility (Cooper *et al.*, 2000). This approach should not be confused with inconsistency or indiosyncracy in rule enforcement. The consistent feature here is respect for individuals, and the recognition that different individuals, with different circumstances, will sometimes need different treatment.

The third condition – that of students needing to feel that they are valued as individuals – in turn receives support from the sense of safety and the quality of relationships that form the two conditions already mentioned. The defining characteristic of this condition is the provision of opportunities for students to experience acknowledgement and reward for their individual qualities and contributions to the school community. This means that formal reward and acknowledgement should be made available for the widest possible range of achievement. Academic achievement is extremely important in school and opportunities for success in this area will be maximised if the curriculum is delivered in ways that take account of the wide variations between individuals' preferred learning styles, and if efforts are made to provide appropriate support for students experiencing difficulties.

The quality of communication among staff and between staff and students is central to the process by which these conditions can be brought about in a school. People feel safe when they are supported by management systems that they see as consistently fair and effective. They feel cared for when they are consulted about their feelings and views, and when there are clear channels available to everyone for making concerns known. They feel valued and willing to contribute to the community when they are given trust and responsibility, and when they can see that they have the potential to influence what goes on. The best way of promoting these conditions in schools is for there to be an ongoing programme of monitoring and consultation, through which staff and students examine the extent to which these conditions are being met and ways in which they can be met more effectively. It is important that there is a formal consultation procedure, such as through questionnaires, as well as informal procedures whereby staff routinely show an interest in students' concerns and views.

These key conditions will be achieved most effectively when:

- school management provides practical and unconditional support for them;
- there is shared commitment among all staff (including support and ancillary staff) to the achievement of these conditions;
- there is at least one member of staff with significant knowledge and understanding of the nature and causes of social, emotional and behavioural problems, including AD/HD.

PARTNERSHIP WITH CHILD AND PARENTS

Schools work best when staff, students and students' families are working co-operatively toward the same goals. The climate of caring and acceptance described in the previous section contributes to co-operative relationships between staff and students, and these relationships can only be strengthened if parents are inducted in a similar way. There is powerful research evidence to show that work with parents plays a crucial role in helping to overcome emotional and behavioural difficulties among school students of all ages (Webster-Stratton, 1999; Henggeler, 1999).

The basis for good working relationships with parents is very similar to that which applies to staff–student relationships, and that is the need for a climate of care and acceptance. Students will work and behave best in situations where teachers and parents are reinforcing the same expectations about school and behaviour. For this to happen there needs to be a clear channel of communication between teachers and parents. Parents' nights can contribute to this, but are inadequate on their own, since, for various reasons, not all parents are willing to attend. This is especially the case for parents of children who have 'not done well' in one way or another. Furthermore, the often tight schedules on which parents' nights have to be run can mean that they are unsuitable occasions for quiet and detailed discussions.

Parents need to be kept informed about what is going on in their children's school in terms of events and developments (such as changes in school and class rules), and they should be invited to contribute to and comment on such developments. Getting parents to agree and 'sign up to' school rules (before their child is guilty of an infringement) can serve as a valuable preventive measure, and, in turn, aid straight-forwardness in dealing with infringements if they occur (Olsen, 1997). Staff–student and staff–parent relations are also likely to benefit from communications from teacher to parent that highlight children's positive social and academic performance.

It is all too often the case that parents of the most difficult children only communicate with the school when difficulties arise. This creates a poor basis for the staff–parent relationship and can lead to the development of negative perceptions on both sides. For this reason it is of great importance for key staff to make contact with the parents of students they teach as early as possible in their acquaintance with the student. This can be achieved through a variety of means, such as:

- inviting small groups of parents to attend the school for informal meetings during school time (Layzell, 1995);
- inviting parents to take part in occasional classes (either as helpers or simply as pupils);

- having a weekly teacher-hosted luncheon to which parents are invited (Webster-Stratton, 1999).

These measures are of course in addition to the incidental meetings that often occur between parents and teachers. Any early positive contact between staff and parents can help to lay the foundations for a relaxed relationship between teacher and parent. This will prove invaluable help in preventing difficulties, and will ease the process of dealing with problems when they do arise.

The teacher–student–parent triangle will undermine the work of the school if teachers and parents see each other as adversaries who only communicate through the student, who in turn may take advantage of this by playing the two sides off against each other. On the other hand, where there is a direct and independent channel of communication between teachers and parents and a co-operative relationship the student cannot play them off. In these circumstances the parent–teacher relationship becomes a foundation supporting the student's individual and social development. This makes the effort required in cultivating good staff–parent relations very worthwhile.

EVALUATING PROGRESS

Evaluation is a vital component of any educational intervention. The process of education, whether it is concerned with academic knowledge or social behaviour, sets out to foster change. In order to assess students' social, emotional and behavioural progress schools may use the following evaluation tools.

The Goodman Strengths and Difficulties Questionnaires

This is a norm-referenced behaviour rating scale (Goodman, 1997). It has 25 items each of which is rated as 'applies'; 'applies somewhat', or 'does not apply'. The 25 items break down into 5 sub-scales (emotional problems; peer difficulties; hyperactivity; conduct problems, and pro-social behaviour. In addition the scale has an 'impact supplement' (Goodman, 1999) which requests information about the perceived seriousness of the child's behaviour in terms of the level of 'burden' that is placed on the child, school and family by the child's difficulties. The scale is designed for use with children and young persons between the ages of 4 and 16, and has a teacher version, a parent version and a student version (for 11–16 year olds only). It is easy to complete (taking approximately 3–5 minutes per child). It is designed primarily as a screening tool for large groups of children, but is also used as a diagnostic tool for individual students with AD/HD (Hill and Cameron, 1999).

This tool provides a snapshot of the nature and range of behaviour problems as well as perceptions of their severity. The 'pro-social' scale is particularly useful in that it enables the recording of positive behaviour.

The TOAD Schedule

This is a simple observation schedule (Goldstein, 1995) that can be used in classrooms to assess the relative frequency of specific behaviour problems associated with AD/HD:

T = talking out of turn
O = out of seat
A = (not paying) attention
D = disrupting others

The schedule is used on a time-sampling basis, using the following procedure:

1. The observer selects up to three students (the target student plus a second student randomly selected, plus a third student perceived to have no problems).
2. The observer records the frequency of TOAD behaviours performed by all three students over the specified time. (e.g. The teacher or LSA (Learning Support Assistant)) observes each of the three students once (e.g.) every 3 minutes, and generates a frequency score for each of the TOAD items.
3. The observer compares the performances of the three students and records this in graphical form.

There are two main purposes to this:

1. It provides comparative, quantitative data on the target student's behaviour as related to other students, and therefore creates an opportunity to test the perception that the target student has 'problems'.
2. It enables quantitative comparison over time, so that improvement or decline can be recorded. The comparative element provides some indication of the effect of the situation (i.e if all three students' behaviour deteriorates this is likely to be because of situational rather than individual factors).

The TOAD schedule can also be used in conjunction with an intervention record, whereby the observer records the timing of specific interventions and plots this against the TOAD score for individual students. If the TOAD score repeatedly declines during periods of intervention it may be hypothesised that the intervention is working.

Interviews

The aim of interviews is to gauge perceptions of progress and beliefs about factors influencing progress. This should include accessing attributions and beliefs about self-efficacy: i.e. do the students, teachers, parents believe that they have any control over or influence on behaviour? If so, what is the nature of that influence? If not, who or what is influential?

Structured Observation

Where specific behaviours are identified as problematic an observational schedule should be designed (see TOAD) to assess frequency of these behaviours performed by the target student and other students (e.g. one perceived to have problems; one perceived not to have problems).

Reflective diary

Recording of personal reflections (of teachers/LSAs/parents/students) about the nature of the target child's progress and the influences on it. It is valuable for subjective, emotive accounts to be included in such diaries. It may also be appropriate to guarantee confidentiality of the diary itself, given that its main purpose is to encourage the diarists to reflect on situations and their own involvement in them. Diarists should be encouraged to talk with confidants about the content of the diary, and, though they should not be required to hand the diary over to a third party, they may be requested to provide generalised summary points, such as an account of whether or not there appears to have been any improvement in the student's behaviour, or whether they have developed any new insights about how to proceed with the intervention programme.

Measures of Educational Progress

This involves the use of national curriculum attainment targets, Standard Assessment Test (SAT) scores, and the results of standardised numeracy and literacy tests.

Sociogram

All students in class are asked to nominate one student with whom they like to play/socialise and/or work. A social 'map' of the class group can be generated from this.

Using the Data

The numerical data generated by some of these instruments (e.g. the Goodman questionnaire) lends itself to some highly sophisticated forms of statistical analysis. Having said this, most schools will find the raw data useful in itself. The Goodman data for example can be presented in graphical form, or as a single global score, or as an individual score for each sub-item. The TOAD schedule, similarly, generates numerical data that can be presented in graphical form. These two measures alone will enable staff to monitor individual students' progress over time and in relation to the wider student group.

A particular advantage of the range of evaluation tools suggested here is that they provide data not only about progress but also about possible targets for intervention. In this way the evaluation process is made formative, because it feeds directly back into the intervention plan. So, if in the course of interviews with parents it is discovered that a particular problem has arisen in the family (e.g. the death of a close relative), steps can be taken at school to protect the student from situations where this may make the student vulnerable. In this situation the qualitative data is of value, not only because it generates information, but also because the process of gathering the data involves the school taking an active interest in the views and concerns of students and their families.

7
AD/HD in the Classroom:
Basic Principles and Practices

Main topics:

- Establishing the right relationship
- The right setting
- Promoting effective learning
- Managing behaviour
- Thinking positively about AD/HD

In this chapter we describe some of ways in which teachers can make learning tasks accessible to students with AD/HD (see also Cooper and Ideus, 1996). Basic principles are:

1. The need for precision and clarity in communicating with the student with AD/HD.
2. The need to protect the student from distraction.
3. The need to protect and nurture the student's sense of self esteem.

ESTABLISHING THE RIGHT RELATIONSHIP

It would be foolish to underestimate the feelings of frustration that teachers sometimes feel when confronted with students who present learning difficulties. There is a natural tendency among human beings to prefer the company of people who are easy to get along with. Teachers, like everyone else, are going to warm to some students more than others, and they are going to have negative feelings about others. These feelings are sometimes going to interact with students' own frustrations and social preferences. And, of course, students are going to like and relate easily to some teachers more than others. These feelings are legitimate and should not be denied. There are good professional reasons, however, why it is important for teachers to aim for a particular kind of relationship with their students which avoids allowing these personal feelings to influence the way in which they interact with one another.

The key point here is that teaching and learning are primarily social processes. They involve a transactional relationship between teacher and learner, in which there is a sharing and exchange of ideas and understanding. Learning depends on the learner's willingness to expose their existing knowledge to the teacher's probes, so that the teacher can accurately assess students' current state of understanding and, therefore, the scope for extending this (Vygotsky, 1987; Bruner and Haste, 1987).

Learning takes place when the teacher creates a situation which enables students to use their existing knowledge to discover new knowledge. A key feature of this teaching process is sometimes referred to as 'scaffolding' (Bruner, 1987). This word captures the essence of the teaching–learning relationship, by emphasising the idea that skilled teaching involves creating structures which students use as platforms from which, like workers on a building site, they create new structures (i.e. knowledge). This also emphasises the active as opposed to passive nature of learning. From the students' perspective, however, this process is fraught with risks.

First there is the danger of exposure: that is, in revealing their existing knowledge they may reveal ignorance or incompetence. Second, there is always the possibility that the teacher's scaffolding is inadequate or inappropriate, thus putting students at risk of failure and humiliation. Students with learning difficulties and/or a history of academic failure feel particularly vulnerable in these respects.

All students learn most effectively in environments where they feel respected and cared for, and where they feel supported (Cooper and McIntyre, 1996). These features form the basis of the relationship of trust that is essential to the learning process. Success in the formal curriculum brings respect and admiration almost automatically in most classrooms. Special care often has to be taken, however, to ensure that students for whom academic success does not come easy are made aware that they are respected and cared for in ways that are essential for the nurturance of their social, personal and educational development.

Dialogue

The basis for effective teacher–student relationships (and all human relationships) is constant, day-to-day dialogue. Dialogue refers not only to verbal interaction, but to the dialogue that goes on in writing between students' written work and teachers' comments. It also refers to subtle messages that are communicated obliquely in the classroom: the public comments a teacher makes to individuals or groups often communicate messages to other students. And whilst dialogue is a two-way process, in the classroom it is the teacher ultimately who sets the tone.

The most important thing about this dialogue is that it should communicate the teacher's empathy and positive regard for the student. It is also important that the teacher be honest and avoids misleading the student about the desirability of anti-social or other negative behaviours. It comes naturally to some teachers to show a personal interest in their students, by asking them questions or sharing humour with them. Non-sarcastic humour is actually a low-key way of expressing positive regard to another person. This dialogue helps the teacher to:

- monitor the student's mood state and feelings about the success or otherwise of the intervention programme
- learn about personal, family and social factors that may influence the student's performance
- indicate ways of extending the student's existing knowledge and understanding
- detect learning difficulties
- develop a positive relationship with the student
- model to the student and others positive modes of interaction.

Tone of voice is important. There are good reasons why AD/HD exasperates teachers and leads them to raise their voices. Students with attentional problems are more forgetful than most children. This is in spite of the fact that schools often run on the basis of expectations about the ability of students to remember things. 'If I've told you once I've told you a thousand times' is not always an unreasonable complaint – though it is a pointless complaint to a person who has difficulty remembering things. The tone, however, that goes with such statements will communicate unambiguous anger and, maybe, personal dislike. For this reason task requirements, even when being repeated for the umpteenth time, should always be communicated as though for the first time, in a calm and measured way.

THE RIGHT SETTING

Students with AD/HD are easily distracted. It is important to ensure that they are seated in the classroom in a place that is relatively free from distraction. This will often mean sitting away from doors, windows, and displays or other items that might cause distraction. Students prone to distraction and inattentiveness should also be seated in a place where the teacher can readily detect if the student is or is not attending and, if necessary, intervene without embarrassing the student or disrupting the lesson. This does not necessarily mean demanding that he or she always sit next the teacher's desk. It is helpful for teachers to consider the ways in which all students are seated in their classrooms, so that all students are available to unobtrusive individual teacher intervention. Having said this, the practicalities and idiosyncracies of some teaching environments mean that compromises have to be made. In these circumstances the teacher has to think very carefully about the seating positions of certain students. Some teachers favour having a number of desks placed up against walls, so that the seated student faces the wall. During periods where students are required to focus on individual work this helps to reduce opportunities for distraction. Task requirements or other reminders can be posted on the wall in front of the student. This approach can be extended by having non-transparent panels placed on either side of the seated child, thus creating a three-sided box (or 'carrell') which reduces both visual and auditory distractions. Having a number of such carrells in a classroom can be useful to all students at different times, but particularly useful to those prone to distraction. Similarly, where feasible, classrooms often benefit from having a 'quiet area' where individuals or small groups of students can go to study in silence.

Floor markings can serve a useful purpose in reminding students to remain at their desks during periods of 'seat work' (i.e. students are not permitted leave the zone which extends 1 foot from their seat which is marked by lines on the floor).

Students and teachers work best in a calm and orderly atmosphere. This is not the same as saying that a quiet classroom is always a good classroom (Weaver, 1994). At the heart of the learning process is social interaction, which often involves verbal communication. So just as measures need to be taken to enable students to experience quietness when it is required, so care has to be taken to manage pupil interaction so that it is constructive. An important point to remember here is that students with AD/HD tend to perform best in pair rather than group situations. This is because in groups there tend to be too many possible distractions, and too much strain placed on the child's limited social skills, thus making group situations over-stimulating.

All children, and particularly those with AD/HD, benefit from clear, predictable, uncomplicated routine and structure. It helps if the day is divided into broad units of time, and that this pattern is repeated daily. Within each block of lesson time there should be a similar breaking down of tasks and activities into sub-tasks/activities. Presenting the student with an enormously detailed list of tasks and sub-tasks should be avoided. An important goal should be to create a simple overarching daily routine that the student will eventually learn by heart. The number of tasks should be kept small, and deadlines should be realistic. Complexities of timetabling and working structures merely confuse students with AD/HD, because a major difficulty that goes with this condition is a poorly developed ability to differentiate between and organise different bits of information. This clearly makes the formal curriculum difficult enough to manage, without having to struggle with the organisational arrangements surrounding the curriculum. Once a workable daily timetable has been established this should be publicly displayed and/or taped to the student's desk or inside their homework diary. Where possible the timetable should be illustrated pictorially. Similarly, clear public signs and colour coding indicating the location of particular resources and as an aid to to finding one's way around the school site can be of enormous benefit to students with AD/HD.

PROMOTING EFFECTIVE LEARNING

It would be a mistake to assume that all students with AD/HD share the same learning characteristics. All students are different, and need to be approached as such, through careful analysis of their individual needs. However, there are certain learning characteristics that crop up in the AD/HD population more commonly than in the general student population. This section deals with some of these characteristics.

Learning Styles

Teachers and students are more satisfied with the effectiveness of teaching and learning when teachers create learning environments that enable students to engage with learning tasks in a variety of ways, according to their preferred learning styles (Cooper and McIntyre, 1996). Learning, by definition, is always about thinking. With this in mind we might draw a distinction between people whose thinking processes are, on the one hand, best stimulated by physical involvement and activity, and those who, on the other hand, respond best to abstract or conceptual input. Kolb (1984: 68–9) further subdivides these types:

1. A preference for learning from *concrete experience* which emphasises feeling over thinking; here and now complexity over theories and generalisations; intuitive over systematic.

2. A preference for *reflective observation* which emphasises understanding over practical application; the ideal over the pragmatic; reflection over action.

3. A preference for *abstract conceptualisations* which emphasises thinking over feeling; theories over here and now complexity; systematic over intuitive.

4. A preference for *active experimentation* which emphasises pragmatic over ideal; doing rather than observing.

People with AD/HD tend to favour the concrete experience and active experimentation learning styles (Wallace and Crawford, 1994). These learning styles are most suited to experiential tasks: that is, where the learning emerges from doing. This means that drama, role play and other practical and imaginative tasks will tend to get the best out of some students. This means that the traditional tendency of many schools to focus on tasks which are essentially reflective, abstract, and text based will discriminate against some students. This is in spite of the fact that much curriculum content can also be approached by using alternative experiential means (see Cooper and McIntyre, 1996 and Cooper and Ideus, 1996).

AD/HD and Creativity

Not all students with AD/HD are especially creative, but there are times when AD/HD characteristics can be associated with creativity. As we have already noted AD/HD is the product of a particular set of cognitive differences which mean that the individual with AD/HD often experiences the world in what most people would see as unusual ways. For many individuals with AD/HD this creates confusion and difficulty, but sometimes it leads to novel and highly creative interpretations and insights of a type associated with 'divergent thinking'. Individuals with AD/HD also sometimes share other characteristics associated with creativity, such as self-centredness; emotional hypersensitivity; impulsiveness, spontaneity, and unpredictability (Crammond, 1994; Jordan, 1992).

Of course being creative is no excuse for bad behaviour. On the other hand creative abilities present the teacher with indications of the kinds of activities that will act as a positive channel for the student's energies. Creative students can often be a valuable resource to the classroom teacher in their ability to offer divergent ways of looking at things or novel approaches (and solutions) to problems. Openly acknowledging and giving status to students' abilities in this area can again help to provide students who might otherwise be marginalised and isolated with a way of becoming positively involved in classroom activities.

Learning Tasks

The particular nature of AD/HD makes it especially important to ensure that the learning task is stimulating for the student. Students with AD/HD do not tend to do well with repetitive tasks. If tasks are not stimulating they will allow the child to become easily distracted. This means that the task should be sharply delineated and highly focused.

Complex tasks will be made accessible if they are broken down into a small number of short steps or instructions. It is important that task instructions are concise and clear with as few sub-parts as possible. Getting individual students to repeat instructions orally, preferably in their own words, can help to ensure that student has registered the instructions. Also, when being given a list of instructions, it is better if each instruction is given and digested before the next instruction is given. Where appropriate, the instructions should be presented in a form that will allow the pupil to retrieve them if he or she forgets, such as in writing and/or in pictorial form. The student should also be encouraged to compose his or her own lists of instructions where this is appropriate. Also, teachers who routinely preview and review tasks help students to know what is expected of them and to make sense of what they are doing. These are also habits that students can usefully be encouraged to carry out for themselves.

Over time the child with AD/HD should be encouraged to tackle tasks of increasing complexity. Initially, however, tasks should be calculated to ensure that the student is able to complete them successfully. The length and complexity of tasks should increase only when the student has shown success with shorter assignments. This is not only important from the viewpoint of skill development, it is also a valuable way of enhancing the student's self-confidence and self-esteem.

The difficulties students with AD/HD often have with sequencing, concentration/distractibility can make writing a very difficult task. Offering students alternative means of presenting knowledge (e.g. through tape, use of an amanuensis, computer, etc.) can help here.

Students with AD/HD respond well to praise and rewards, which are applied when they achieve a desired target. Small and immediate rewards are invariably more effective than long-term or delayed rewards. It is important to remember that students with AD/HD are easily distracted, therefore, rewards should not be overly elaborate or likely to overshadow the task in any way. Rewards need to be as immediate as possible, since students with AD/HD often have problems with thinking outside of their immediate time frame. It should also be remembered that students with AD/HD often require more specific and more frequent feedback on their work performance than most pupils. This is partly due to their memory and attention problems as well as a by-product of low self-esteem.

Timing

Students with AD/HD often have particular problems with maintaining a sense of time. In fact the experience of AD/HD has sometimes been described as feeling like being cut off from the past and future, as if the individual is only aware of the present moment. This is a serious problem when we think of the fact that many of us use our sense of time to enable us to 'put up' with uncomfortable, boring or stressful situations. Knowing that this tedious film/lecture/meeting/lesson/visit only has so many days, hours or minutes to run helps us to calculate whether or not the situation is bearable. On the other hand, not knowing how much longer we have to endure discomfort can lead us to give up at the first opportunity.

Teachers exploit students' sense of time when they say things like: 'as soon as you have finished this difficult piece of writing you can do X' (i.e. something that the students prefer). For some students an offer like this acts as a motivator. It indicates that the sole task is to arrive at the desired product. Of course, when teachers do this they often have to remind students of quality requirements, and either state or imply the consequences of failure to produce work of the required quality. Again, this exploits the students' abilities to think forwards and backwards. If (based on their experience) they believe the promised consequences of poor effort, they will be influenced by them. For some students the equation presented by these combined factors leads them to abandon the idea of trying to finish the task quickly. This kind of intervention works best with students whose need is to have their powers of application stimulated. It is often completely counterproductive for many students with AD/HD. In these circumstances they will be inclined to abandon the task as soon as possible, with little consideration for consequences, particularly if the consequences are not immediate.

Students with attentional difficulties require support in structuring their time. This means that prescribed time limits are often more effective than open-ended tasks for these students. Teachers sometimes employ timing devices, such as clocks or sand-timers to help students gauge the passage of time. The visual quality of sand-timers, which come in different sizes for different lengths of time, seems particularly effective for some students because they provide a physical representation of the passage of time. The effectiveness of this intervention, however, is contingent on the appropriateness and structure of the task, on the time frame being matched to the task, and on mindfulness of the problem of 'recess deprivation' (see above).

MANAGING BEHAVIOUR

Behaviour management inevitably plays an important part in the education of students with attention and activity problems. It is tempting sometimes to see behaviour as the main problem, and, therefore, the main focus of intervention. This approach can be counter-productive. Within the school setting behaviour problems are almost always best dealt with, first and foremost, as educational problems, with specific behaviour management interventions being used to supplement and support educational strategies of the type referred to above.

Furthermore, students with learning and behaviour difficulties often have emotional difficulties as well. They lack confidence. They associate school with failure and rejection. They may find it especially difficult to relate to adult authority figures, for the simple reason that they have experienced consistent setbacks in meeting the expectations of significant adults in their lives. These problems are sometimes compounded when they observe peers, younger siblings, relatives or acquaintances achieving adult approval with apparent effortlessness. This means that programmes directed at the control of behaviour will be most effective if they are embedded in the context of a school environment that encourages students to feel individually valued and cared for (see above). Where such a caring context does not exist, the behaviour management programme may not only fail but be experienced by students as provocative (Cooper *et al.*, 2000).

Having said this, there is high-quality evidence to support the view that behavioural strategies can be very effective in enabling students with AD/HD to conform to rules. This applies both with and without the aid of medication (Hinshaw, Klein and Abikoff, 1998).

Maintaining An Educational Focus

Before embarking on a programme of behavioural intervention it is important to bear a few things in mind that will ultimately contribute to the effectiveness of the programme. In the face of severe behaviour problems it is understandable that teachers sometimes become attached to the idea that if they could simply stop Liam or Courtney from behaving so badly then things would be fine. Whilst there is undoubted truth in this view, it can make the intervention programme educationally counter-productive, by encouraging the emphasis to be placed on bad behaviour rather than on promoting good, educationally productive behaviour.

Interventions should emphasise positive, desirable outcomes rather than the negative, unwanted behaviour. This means that targets for improvement should focus on academic products and performance (e.g. work completion) rather than specific behaviours (e.g. remaining in seat). Furthermore, goals should stress what is desired rather than what is not desired. DuPaul and Stoner's (1994) 'dead man' test is useful here. In order to apply this test the teacher simply has to ask if a dead person could carry out the required behaviour. If the answer is yes then it means that the requirement is for the absence of behaviour. Negative expectations of this kind are likely to be problematic for all children. Behavioural requirements should, where possible, be positive in the sense that they tell students what they should be doing, rather than what they shouldn't be doing.

All of the interventions described below involve communication between teacher and student. We suggest that a rule of thumb might be to make behavioural interventions as non-disruptive to the flow of lessons as possible. For this reason (1) the management of behaviour in the public environment of the classroom should, ideally, exploit the non-verbal channel of communication. And (2) where verbal intervention is necessary, emphasis should, as much as possible, be aimed at the positive reinforcement of desired behaviour, rather than the condemnation of unwanted behaviour. These two suggestions will contribute to the positive climate of the classroom by keeping the focus of classroom discourse pleasant and positive, as well as allowing more classroom talk to be devoted to teaching and learning and less to complaining.

A further point to bear in mind is that individual differences between students mean that a strategy which works well with one student may not work so well with another. In choosing strategies, therefore, the individual characteristics of students should be borne in mind. Once a strategy has been selected, however, it should not be abandoned simply because it does not achieve the desired effect immediately. Very few interventions work that quickly. Once a strategy has been decided upon it should be put into practice for a predetermined period of time, over which its effectiveness is measured using approaches described in the 'evaluation' section above, or similar quantitative measures.

Behavioural Interventions

Common behavioural interventions, if applied with diligence and consistency, can be helpful in establishing and reinforcing behavioural requirements and boundaries. From a teacher's perspective the key principle underpinning behavioural approaches is that we can influence the extent to which a pattern of behaviour is repeated by manipulating the amount and the nature of attention we give it. The following behavioural approaches, when applied in support of a clear set of sensible rules (see Chapter 6), are of proven effectiveness in enabling students with AD/HD to conform to rules.

Ignore–Rules–Praise (Wheldall and Merrett, 1987). This involves the teacher in ignoring a behaviour which infringes a rule whilst, simultaneously, reinforcing behaviour which complies with the same rule (see Box 7.1). In the behavioural sense, ignoring is the removal of attention that might act as reinforcement. It is not an act of rudeness whereby a student's attempts at positive interaction with the teacher are rejected.

The Ignore–Rules–Praise Strategy

Example

The Raise Your Hand Rule: When the teacher asks the whole class a question students are to raise their hands if they know the answer and not speak until asked by the teacher.

1. Teacher asks the class: 'Who can tell me the name of an extinct animal?'

2. Sara calls out: 'Dodo!'

3. Teacher ignores Sara's answer, and says to Anne, who has raised her hand: 'Well done Anne for remembering the raise your hand rule. What's your answer?'

Box 7.1

Time-out: this involves the student being sent to a place where he/she is required to remain for a short specified period (3–5 minutes) when he or she is misbehaving, where he/she will not receive stimulation or attention. It should be clearly explained to the student (i) why it is being done, with direct reference to the offence, and (ii) what it is intended to achieve (e.g. to give time for reflection, time to cool off). It is also important that when the time-out period is over the teacher responds to the student with warmth and acceptance to indicate that the 'offence' has now been dealt with and can be put in the past in favour of current and more positive pursuits. It is important of course that warmth and acceptance is not only shown to the student in relation to time-out. If this is the case such attention will reinforce to the student the desirability of behaving in ways that lead to time-out.

A sand-timer, or other timing device, can be utilised for this approach.

Some teachers employ a non-verbal card system as part of this approach, whereby a yellow card is shown to the student or placed on their desk, as a warning that they are beginning to engage in behaviour that might lead to time-out. A red card is then shown, which means 'go to time-out'.

A variation on the time-out theme is sometimes applied in which it is the student who decides when he/she needs time-out. Again a card system can be used to communicate this to the teacher, so that undue attention is not drawn to the situation.

Behavioural contracts: these are another way of establishing expectations, discussing them with the child and reinforcing them. Here an agreement is made between the teacher and student, or among students, which establishes clear behavioural expectations, states how these are to be achieved and relates their achievement to particular rewards. Rewards should be short-term and low-key (see above). Sanctions are also specified for failure to achieve goals and the recurrence of specific negative behaviours. Such contracts should be brief, highly specific and expressed in ways which the student clearly understands. Requiring the student to compose the contract in his or her own words, for the approval of all signatories to the contract, is an effective measure with some students.

Token economies: this involves the giving of tokens, in the form of points, stickers, or other 'currency', as rewards for positive rule-compliant behaviour. These tokens are then exchanged for a more concrete reward, such as a preferred activity or more tangible reward.

Preferred activities (e.g. working on a computer) are usually more effective rewards (in the sense of being long-lasting and powerful) than concrete rewards (e.g. sweets). It is the student's preference that counts here. For example, not all students see working on the computer as a treat: this may be especially true of a child who makes use of a computer as a regular part of their learning programme (as is the case for many children with literacy difficulties and AD/HD). For this reason, appropriate rewards are likely to be effectively identified through negotiation between teacher and student. This can lead to the development of a 'rewards menu' which contains a *variety* of possible rewards which can be used to avoid the staleness and boredom that might result from the repetition of the same reward over time.

Negative consequences, in the form of mild, non-physical punishment, can sometimes be effective. They should be used sparingly, be clearly focused and highly specific. For example, mild reprimands for being off-task will be most effective when they involve a reminder of the task requirement. Thus it is better to say: "Please, stop talking and get back to reading page three of your history booklet", rather than, "Please get on with your work". Their effectiveness will also be enhanced in classrooms where teachers are habitually positive in their behaviour towards children. It is interesting to note that students do not like to be told off by teachers who hold them in high regard; conversely, students often find it difficult to accept praise from teachers who habitually treat them with contempt or disrespect.

Priming helps motivate students with AD/HD in a positive sense. This involves previewing with the student the task and the likely rewards of successful completion.

THINKING POSITIVELY ABOUT AD/HD

Children with AD/HD often come to be locked into cycles of negativity, whereby it seems that everything they do leads to rejection or reprimand. Teachers also can sometimes find themselves trapped into perpetuating these cycles. Reframing is a technique that has many valuable applications, especially when dealing with behavioural problems. It involves finding a new and positive way of thinking about a child's problem behaviour, and has the effect of helping the teacher to break cycles of negativity.

Although the reframing technique may at first appear to defy common sense, it should be pointed out that it is based on practices used by some clinical psychologists to great success with very severe emotional and behavioural disorders. These practices were first adapted for educational settings by Molnar and Lindquist (1989) in the US, and were applied to behavioural problems in the UK by Cooper and Upton (1990) and Cooper, Smith and Upton (1994).

The approach stresses the importance of framing all students' behaviour as positively as possible. This is not the same as condoning unwanted or undesirable behaviour. The purpose of the technique is to help the teacher to develop ideas about the *positive* ways in which children might use certain of their behavioural characteristics; in particular, those which are seen as a source of problems. The technique also allows the teacher to indicate that although a behaviour may not be appropriate in one situation, there may be situations to which the behaviour is highly or at least more appropriate. This can have important consequences for:

- students' self-esteem
- the development of co-operative teacher–student relationships in class
- changing behaviour.

Reframing undesirable behaviours in positive ways helps students to believe that:

- the teacher likes them
- the teacher cares about them.

In using this technique it is important to avoid communicating approval of undesirable behaviour. It may well be the case that some forms of behaviour, such as those involving violence, may not lend themselves to this reframing. It is important to use the technique where it has a chance of being effective, and where it will be productive and convincing. Sometimes it may be appropriate to use the reframing technique in a way that also indicates a mild disapproval of the current behaviour. This can be done by providing a positive reframing of the unwanted behaviour and then indicating that there are situations, other than the present one, in which these qualities are more appropriately displayed.

For reframing to be successful it must be:

- convincing, in that it fits the facts of the situation as student and teacher see them
- done in a genuine way (without sarcasm)
- communicated in a way that shows respect and care for the student.

Some negative and positive ways of framing characteristics of AD/HD (based on Hartmann, 1993):

Negative	Positive
Distractible	Alert to what is going on
Poor planner; disorganised; impulsive	Flexible; ready to change strategy quickly
Distorted sense of time	Tireless when motivated
Impatient	Keen to get on with things
Difficulty converting words into concepts	Visual/concrete thinker
Has difficulty following directions	Independent
Daydreamer	Bored by mundane tasks/imaginative
Acts without considering consequences	Willing and able to take risks; fearless
Lacking in social skills	Single-minded in pursuit of goals

These are some possible positive reframes for common classroom problems:

Negative	Positive
Being out of seat too frequently	energetic and lively
Deviating from what the rest of the class is supposed to be doing	independent, inquisitive, individualistic
Talking out of turn or calling out	keen/impatient to contribute
Being aggressive towards classmate	sensitive, emotional, passionate
Losing and forgetting equipment	unmaterialistic
Handing in homework late or not at all	perfectionist; unable to get started because of high standards

Put simply students with AD/HD (like all students) perform most effectively when tasks are tailored to harness their positive skills and abilities. They are also likely to be more motivated when teachers and others behave towards them in ways that are positive and geared to enhancing their self-esteem.

Part 3:
AD/HD in Action:
Case Studies

In this section we turn to a range of case studies. The intention of this section is to present examples of the many different ways in which AD/HD manifests itself in the classroom situation. This is important because, as the teacher who works with a student with AD/HD will discover, the core symptoms of AD/HD are often only part of a constellation of difficulties that the student presents. The examples that are offered in this section will not cover all of the possible combinations of problems presented by students with AD/HD. The examples do, however, reflect something of the variety of combinations, and indicate practical ways of dealing with them in the school setting. These cases are all based on first-hand experience of working with students with AD/HD in a school setting. All of the students dealt with here attended the same specialist day school which catered for fifty-two boys and girls between the ages of 8 and 18.

The school is an independent school for students who fall in the average to above average range in terms of cognitive ability, but who have learning difficulties such as dyslexia and AD/HD. The maximum class size is 12 students, and individualised teaching is provided. A strong emphasis is placed on helping students to develop the skills of self-directed learning. The school operates a dual curriculum, enabling students to work towards either GCSE examinations or the US High School Diploma.

8
The Different Faces
of AD/HD

As we showed in Part 1 of this book the formal diagnostic criteria for AD/HD (APA, 1994) identify three main sub-types of AD/HD. In this chapter we propose our own wider list of sub-types. It is important to stress that these typings are not based on a controlled study of the population of children with AD/HD, rather they are based on first-hand experience of working with students with the diagnosis in a school setting. This means that they are based largely on the range of students who happen to have been encountered by one of the authors (FO) in a career spanning some 15 years, much of it working specifically with students diagnosed with AD/HD. It should be stressed that these typings are not wholly original, and overlap in some respects with those proposed by other authors (e.g. Kewley, 1999; Barkley, 1990). Unlike other sub-typings, however, they are presented specifically from an educator's perspective. We hope that the value of this approach is that it provides fellow professionals with concrete examples, couched in the language of teaching, that they will be able to relate to their experience. In the following chapters each of these sub-types will be elaborated in the form of individual case studies.

THE TYPES

AD/HD with Oppositional Defiance

This is the oppositional angry student who seems to have given up caring in the belief that the whole world is against them. This student has become enveloped in a progressively thickening cocoon of defiance which acts as a defensive barrier against outside forces, particularly parents and teachers. This pattern sometimes begins to develop in the later years of the primary phase, and is most common in the adolescent years. It is marked by argumentativeness, verbal aggression and a tendency to react in an 'over the top' manner to what others see as minor issues.

This student's defensive wall makes the vulnerable person within not only difficult to help, but difficult to see. It is so easy to come into conflict with this person that the symptoms of AD/HD which lie at the core of a range of learning difficulties are easily reinterpreted as being the product of the student's basic oppositionality : 's/he could do it if s/he tried.'

AD/HD with Detachment

This is the student who, on the surface, appears to be completely lethargic, seeming to prefer their own strange and distant world to the one occupied by most of the rest of the class. Here passive resistance stands in for defiance and many of these students have effectively given up. This student appears to be completely unresponsive to positive reinforcement or sanctions, and has opted out of trying to achieve or attempt educational or social targets.

This student is not as objectionable as the oppositional/defiant type, but shares an underlying unhappiness, and is equally unrewarding to the teacher; the two types look very different from each other but share the same impenetrability. The teacher has to guard against simply ignoring the detached/defeated student, and has to work very hard to make any kind of positive connection.

AD/HD with Impulsivity

This is the bright and breezy student whose attitude and zest for life remain undiminished despite problems at school or at home. They may come across as 'dizzy' or seemingly oblivious to the difficulties around them. It is possible that these children have grown up in an understanding and supportive social environment. As a result they retain a positive attitude and enthusiasm in spite of the learning difficulties that stem from their hyperactivity and impulsiveness.

The problem here is that the teacher may be tempted to 'let sleeping dogs lie'. This student is contented, undemanding and often pleasant. Other, more demanding students may command more immediate attention.

AD/HD with Obsessions

This is the student who really appears to have a very personal agenda, literally, to the point of obsession. They seem quite happy, so long as they can devote their time to their specific areas of interest, be it, for example, train timetables, bus routes, dinosaurs, key rings, or curtains. They will appear to be completely absorbed by their special interest to the exclusion of all else. They will often distance themselves from group activities and sometimes they may have a number of quirks or problematic gross motor movements with their hands and/or facial expressions.

The challenge for the teacher is to tread the fine line between indulging the student, for the sake of a quiet life, and utilising obsessions in the educational process.

AD/HD with Learning Difficulties

This is the student who has AD/HD along with a specific learning difficulty such as an auditory processing problem or dyslexia. This combination is a 'double whammy' that can make it often difficult to decide what is causing the student's learning problems. Such students are obviously at risk in school for although the learning difficulty may be identified and materials/specialist teaching supplied, the students often lack the basic listening and other study skills commonly expected in the classroom. They may have problems of inattentiveness and disorganisation. They may be hypoactive as in the Inattentive form of AD/HD and more often than not can be girls who come across as unmotivated, distracted and forgetful, prone to losing things. Often too they become the recipients of additional unhelpful criticism as teachers/parents mistakenly blame the failure of remediation efforts on the child's lack of motivation.

AD/HD with High Ability

This is the student with AD/HD who also reveals evidence of unusually high ability. These students will rarely realise their apparent ability in their classroom and examination performance. A central problem for them is their difficulty in focusing or paying attention to detail when the lesson/material is of little interest to them. A common refrain of such students is: 'It's boring.' They lack the often unrecognised skill possessed by many learners to 'dig in' and keep their focus when confronted with learning tasks that hold little intrinsic interest for them. Whereas most students, using a scale of 1 to 10 to represent interest level, can cope with levels of 2 or 3 before 'switching off', the student we are talking about here only engages when the interest level is at 9 or 10.

This problem is not the product of willfulness or lack of motivation, but simply the result of severe difficulties in regulating attention. These students simply need a higher level of stimulation than most to retain their engagement. If the work presented appears to them to be unstimulating they will become de-motivated and lose interest in school. Unfortunately, this genuine difficulty can be compounded by that not uncommon adolescent phenomenon of work avoidance. In these circumstances difficulties with attending can be exploited as a ploy whereby *everything* is dismissed as 'boring'. As a result these students can sometimes appear to be stubborn and cocky, and, in so doing, mask their underlying attentional problems. In these circumstances an unhelpful conflict can develop between teacher and student.

AD/HD with Conduct Disorder

This is the student who, in addition to attentional and activity problems, exhibits socially unacceptable behaviours which may include lying, violence towards others, theft and damage to property. This student will tend to exhibit poor attention skills but may show less obvious signs of impulsivity than other students with AD/HD. This student may appear to be more premeditated in his/her actions, sometimes engaging in actions guaranteed to provoke a reaction from peers or teachers. This can be the most stressful and disheartening student to deal with. As in other cases, the negative, and in this case offensive, surface behaviours can mask the underlying cognitive problems, and lead to unnecessary and unhelpful conflict between teacher and student.

AD/HD Combined Type

This is the student who represents a hybrid combination of some or even all of the above. In a condition characterised by erratic and unpredictable behaviour this student stands out as being especially erratic and unpredictable. The challenge for teachers is to remain calm and consistent in their approach towards this student.

CONCLUSION

As we noted earlier, these eight types are not intended to be exhaustive. They represent a range of the ways in which AD/HD manifests itself in real classrooms. These students are in fact in classrooms as we write, or have only recently left school. The following chapters will give some insight into what has actually been done with these students in those classrooms.

9
AD/HD with Oppositional Defiance

Dan really did not want to be at school – that much was very evident when he first walked into the Head's office. Sullen and aggressive, his first words to the Headmaster were: 'That tie you are wearing does not match your shirt!'

Now most people will probably see this as somewhat rude. The Head certainly did. But for Dan it was his first thought and 'boom!' it was said without any concern for how it might sound or how it might be received. Fortunately, the Head was not a vain man. In fact he mentally noted that the boy had a point, as today there was indeed a marked lack of co-ordination between shirt and tie that was unusual even for him. As the meeting progressed, however, it became evident that Dan's comment was not an isolated social blunder, but rather an example of what emerged as part of a pattern of defiance.

'So why do you think you have problems at school?' asked the Head, somewhat carefully, trying not to be distracted by the fact that Dan was leaning back on his chair at a dangerous angle, and studying the ceiling whilst tugging on the cord hanging down by the window blind.

'I don't have problems, it's them that have the problems!' Dan snapped back in reply, eyes still on the ceiling.

'OK,' thought the Head. 'So this is not a great start.'

The tour of the school was not much better as feet were dragged, posters on the wall were pulled, and Dan's communication with his accompanying parents was at best fractious. However, Dan and the school did accept each other, and after two years the Head and staff at the school felt that they had got a handle on the way in which Dan works and thinks. Several incidents seem to stand out which illustrate important things about Dan, and students like him.

Overreaction

One day Dan was asked to leave class for talking too much. When a senior teacher went to talk to him about the incident, Dan became extremely agitated, aggressive and violent, and took a great deal of calming down. The teacher felt his response to be massively out of proportion to the initial problem. Once he had calmed down the teacher asked him to go back into class. Dan seemed surprised at this, saying: 'Doesn't this mean I will be getting kicked out of school?'

Now it was the teacher's turn to be surprised. When he explained to Dan that there was no possibility of his being excluded, it was as if a tremendous weight was suddenly lifted off his shoulders. Dan simply slumped in his chair and became calmer still and contrite.

A way of making sense of Dan's behaviour, in this situation, is to think of it in terms of Dan's style of thinking. In responding to being sent from the classroom he had leapt at least four steps beyond what anyone else was thinking. This was the result of a combination of his sense of insecurity, inspired by past experiences of exclusion, and his lateral, grasshopper way of thinking that is characteristic of AD/HD.

Students, such as Dan, hate alteration of routine, and are threatened and bewildered by change in general: exclusion is rarely an effective intervention for students with AD/HD, but more often an admission of failure on the part of the school.

Dangers of Rigidity

Whilst predictable routine is important, teachers should avoid needless rigidity. An incident involving Dan illustrates this point. One day, during a supervised study period, a teacher noticed that Dan was working on the wrong assignment. He had two unrelated assignments to complete during this period, a Maths assignment and an English assignment, and there was ample time for both. His teacher had given instructions that the Maths assignment should be completed before the English assignment. Dan, however, had decided to do the English assignment first. He was working diligently at this when the supervising teacher realised what was happening. Now there are two ways this could have been handled. The first was to advise the student accordingly and the second was to leave well alone and advise him after he completed the first assignment. After all, both assignments needed to be completed and it shouldn't have mattered in which order this happened. Unfortunately, the teacher chose to advise Dan that he was working on the wrong assignment and that he should stop this and begin the other assignment. This led to a severe tantrum, which resulted in no work being done. The wrong option had been chosen by the teacher, for, in retrospect, no good reason.

Self-Control isn't Easy, but it is Possible

On another day Dan, having been told that he had lost two weeks of privileges on a Monday morning, instead of exploding in the classroom in a furious rage, which had been a typical response in the past, suppressed his anger and frustration until he arrived home that night.

When Dan arrived home he dashed through the house like, as his parents put it, 'a bat out of hell'. He stormed up the stairs and slammed the door of his bedroom. He then savagely tore down the calendar from his wall and viciously crossed off fourteen days while circling the fifteenth in a frenzy. Then we are told he calmly put the calendar back on the wall and padded downstairs for dinner in an almost relaxed and calm manner. These experienced parents carefully avoided asking whether Dan had enjoyed a good day assuming rightly that this would be pushing the situation a little far.

From the school's point of view this story meant that the system was starting to work. Dan was beginning to internalise the controls that the school was applying through its routines. The fact that Dan had infringed a school rule and incurred a punishment was not so important as the fact that he had clearly accepted the punishment without a tantrum, in spite of the fact that it upset him. The really positive thing was that he had managed his frustration and released it in a controlled way without taking it out on other people. This was the product of months of educational training.

Playing to Dan's Strengths

Dan was a student of many contrasts who tended tulips in his back yard but had been regarded as a terror of the classroom in his previous school. At his new school he became one of the students who was often used to help host parents' evenings at the school. He performed these duties so well (for the princely fee of £3.50 per hour) that some staff were frankly amazed. It seemed that being given genuine trust and responsibility (and not forgetting the tangible reward) helped Dan to focus, to control his impulses and to organise himself and others. In his final few years at the school he was recruited for a number of jobs including escorting younger students to and from school, and scoring for the basketball team. All of this seems far removed from that first meeting with the Head, and is a clear indication of the progress he has made.

Understanding Dan

Students like Dan, who combine defiance with AD/HD often appear at first sight to be the toughest type of student to manage. The main issue for teachers and other adult supervisors is to remain calm and not to lose their temper with the child. Dan's most challenging characteristics are anger, aggressiveness, intolerance of others, and an apparent unwillingness to take responsibility for his actions. One thing one has to remember about a student like Dan is that the ever present (all too human) temptation to show one's frustration with him and to raise one's voice in anger is about the worst thing one can do. This will almost always lead to confrontation and explosive consequences.

The defiant student has pendulum-like mood swings, sometimes shifting swiftly from high opposition to what appears like puppy dog compliance and sorrow for actions. There were times, after he had been at the school for a while, when Dan would sometimes seem like a wounded animal, craving comfort. This more vulnerable side of Dan revealed the hurt and pain that underlay his anger and defiance, but only emerged after he developed a sense of security and trust in staff.

As in all the other cases we will discuss, the key with Dan was trying to understand things from his point of view. His experience of schooling had been very negative. For him the sound of the alarm clock on Monday meant the beginning of another week, of another term, of another year of hell. As a result when he did manage to pull the sheets from over his head he often went to school with the mindset of giving as good as he got. It was only when he went to a school where his underlying learning problems (i.e. AD/HD) were addressed that he began to drop his defiant façade.

Strategies

Beneath the troubled exterior Dan was a student, like most others, who really wanted to succeed in school. The problem for Dan was that for many years success eluded him. The frustrating thing was that it was not that he didn't know how to do the things needed for school success, it was more of a problem of not being well enough organised to do them when they were required to be done. Often by the time he had thought about doing something, either the times had passed for doing it, or he had completed the task in a half-baked way. The school environment often finds it difficult to deal with students like this.

Dan was helped by providing him with a number of key support facilities, many of which are offered to all students attending the school where he spent the final 3 years of compulsory education. These are:

- a structured work and leisure schedule

- a differentiated curriculum

- assignment of Mentor/Advocate

- a behavioural contract tied to positive conseqences and sanctions

- forward planning for life after school

- multi-professional support, including consideration of medical intervention.

An example, however, of the way an extremely simple procedure can sometimes help is illustrated under the heading of 'a differentiated curriculum'. Staff noticed that Dan was having tremendous problems during Art on a Friday afternoon even though he was fairly good at the subject and seemed favourably disposed towards it. In looking into this more deeply however it was found that the main problem occurred during the second of the double-period class. Staff thought that perhaps he needed a change of scenery and company for the second lesson. It was found that by simply taking Dan into an empty classroom, where he was supervised by a teacher who was on a non-contact period led to dramatic improvements.

For Dan and other Defiant Students some other strategies to be used include:

- Teach the student words or phrases to use in specific situations of stress and/or frustration to enable the development of appropriate ways to communicate displeasure or anger.

- Provide the student with a quiet place to work free of stimuli.

- Make certain that the student understands the consequences of inappropriate behaviour.

- Reduce the emphasis on competition. Repeated failure may result in anger and frustration. Emphasise individual success rather than winning or beating other students.

- Modify or adjust situations which contribute to 'explosive' outbursts.

- Modify groupings to determine the best combination for the student.

- Maintain visibility to and from the student (make sure you can see him/her and s/he can see you easily and clearly).

- Make sure tasks are given at the student's ability level and possibly reduce the number of tasks.

- Make use of predetermined signals.
- Avoid arguing with the student and avoid confrontations.
- Be consistent in expectations and consequences of behaviour.
- Do not criticise. When correcting the student be honest yet supportive.
- Communicate with parents (notes, phone calls) on both positive and negative situations.
- Have a parent join you at school for a day to sit in class with the child.

Finally

Dan is remembered by school staff as one of the toughest students they ever had at the school. He stayed for over three years and there were many ups and downs in that time. When he left in 1999 there were a few more grey-haired staff than there were before he arrived, and at least one suspected ulcer. By and large, however, he represents a success story. Currently he is attending a junior college in the USA. He may have given up tending tulips, but the school staff firmly believe that many of the strategies he learned at the school will stand him in good stead for many years to come.

10
AD/HD with Detachment

The detached student is like an iceberg floating in the ocean. He or she presents a chilly exterior, keeping much hidden from view, even from those who would help them.

Finding a Channel for Communication

Alfie was one such student. He was 13 when he first came to the school. He experienced a range of problems, many of which seemed to relate back to the enormous difficulty he seemed to experience in getting to school on time in the morning. School staff tried positive reinforcement and various punishments to no avail. There was a shared sense among staff that they were just not getting through to Alfie. He was an enigma. Punishment and rewards were met with the same blank indifference. It wasn't that Alfie was defiant or aggressive; he was simply unresponsive. The staff were exasperated but determined not to give up. Sooner or later they would make a breakthrough – they hoped. Eventually their patience paid off.

For want of anything better, a pattern had emerged whereby, when he was late for school, Alfie was required to spend his morning break in detention with a senior member of staff, in the member of staff's office. One of the purposes of these detentions was to work with Alfie on the development of a plan of action to deal with the lateness problem. It was during one of these detentions when the member of staff was surprised at a sudden breach in Alfie's wall of apathy.

The cause of this event was a country and western song that happened to be playing in the office on this occasion. Alfie groaned, saying: 'I hate this music!' His animated disgust did not subside until the offending song had finished. From this point on country and western CDs became part of the staff member's office equipment and when Alfie was late, he spent his breaktime in the room to the sound of Garth Brooks, and similar country and western heroes. When it was suggested that the detention might be extended to compulsory attendance at line-dancing classes after school, Alfie was very rarely late again.

This may sound flippant. The fact is that Alfie needed an experience that would be stimulating enough to create change. The country and western music simply created the desired 'jolt'.

Progress can be Deceptive

As the ball sailed over the fence of the five-a-side football pitch and towards the railway line Alfie impulsively clambered over the broken wood and rusting barbed wire. This was in spite of the protestations of the newly qualified sports teacher, who was teaching the lesson, to 'stop and stay where you are'. Overshadowing these verbal demands the other students applauded and encouraged him to return the ball so as to continue the game.

Once the ball was returned to our now cheering students, Alfie appeared to be stranded as he was unable to make his way up the vertical incline of the bank. As a result he needed to retreat back down to the tracks in search of a better path. That was the moment when the train stopped. The teacher, and Alfie's fellow students, lost sight of him as he was escorted into the cabin by the angry train driver.

Soon after the transport police phoned the school to say that they had Alfie in the local railway office, and were thinking of charging him for his reckless behaviour. The Head was embarrassed but also relieved. At least Alfie had been compliant with the railway authorities. Eventually after much discussion with the angry police the Head convinced them that this was an incident that would not happen again and that the school would take the necessary measures. Alfie was released back to the school with a caution.

For the school staff, Alfie, and his parents, this had been one of those occasions which no one could have foreseen. The fact that this incident could have ended in tragedy led to some soul-searching on the part of the school. Was the school the right place for Alfie? On balance it was decided that he should stay at the school, because, in spite of the continuing problems, progress was being made with Alfie. He was beginning to respond to school in positive ways that were completely unprecedented in his school career. The lateness problem was the prime example of this. Also, there was a definite sense that Alfie had been somewhat chastened by his brush with the British Transport Police. So too was the school, which introduced specific measures to guard against a repetition of this incident.

The Importance of Perseverence and Flexibility

'It's like walking through treacle,' complained the teacher when describing Alfie's habit of handing in some good work mixed with unfinished or missing assignments. Alfie, whose under-active (i.e. hypoactive) learning style left him unfazed by any negative consequences, was constantly a challenge to all who came into contact with him. This meant that a key quality required by staff who worked with Alfie was perseverence.

In Alfie's world 'time' and 'consequences' were alien, amorphous qualities. The relationship of cause and effect was similarly something that did not hold meaning for him. This made it difficult for him to relate to the rules and guidelines of the school day. It was not that Alfie broke rules deliberately, it was just that it seldom occurred to him that there was a set of rules to be obeyed in the first place.

At times it seemed that whatever system the staff might try for some of the other students would not work for Alfie, as in the example of the lunchtime privilege system.

This system was a major incentive for students of the ages of 15+ who would be allowed off campus during morning break in the event of task completion and compliance with the rules and guidelines of the school. It was a major prize and successful strategy with many students, but not for Alfie. He didn't want to leave the campus during this time but instead preferred to work on his computer game skills or to sit staring alone into space. Because the privilege meant nothing to him, he had no reason to follow the pertinent rules and guidelines. This was becoming a real problem for staff.

After some discussion it was decided to take a lateral approach. Instead of treating the off-campus time as a privilege for Alfie, it was decided to make it compulsory. The privilege for him would be to be allowed to remain on campus. At first some staff feared that this might devalue the privilege for other students. But this did not turn out to be the case. They valued the privilege for its own sake. And, more to the point, they were well aware of the fact that it was not, by Alfie, experienced as a privilege: quite the opposite. Initially this worked well, as Alfie was much more successful with his productivity and punctuality in order to earn the privilege of being allowed back on campus during breaktime on some days. However, things returned to the old routine after a couple of weeks, and the staff soon discovered that Alfie had changed his tune, and now he had experienced it, he liked being off campus! The solution to this was simple: from this point on Alfie would be subject to the same system as everyone else and he would have to earn the privilege of being off campus.

This illustrates a number of key points. First it shows the need to be responsive to the student. Eventually students will tell us what motivates them and what does not, so long as we are vigilant. Second, first-hand experience is more powerful than abstract ideas: Alfie did not know that being off campus was a reward until he experienced it first hand.

General Strategies

The following strategies were employed to support Alfie in school:

- mandatory attendance at homework club and a second set of text books at home
- use of headsets in class during individualised work and forward seat placement away from windows, blinds, etc.
- proactive use of computers/calculators in senior years for work completion
- mentor/advocate to concentrate on organisational skills
- counsellor to work on socialisation skills
- medication options to be considered.

The laptop computer that Alfie was able to use in his GCSE years gave both him and staff tremendous support in getting his work completed in class. The computer meant that he was able to retain his concentration skills more readily and it allowed him to type his information rather than writing it on sheets of paper. This was a definite advantage for a student with good keyboard skills but slow and laborious handwriting, as well as poor organisational skills. This is not to say that laptop computers are the key to everything: these too can be lost, as can the data they hold! They can create other problems too.

One day we had a major altercation between two students in the Year 11 class, which included Alfie and another student. This was a little unusual because Alfie did not often find himself in conflict with other students but you could see at this time that both of them were quite worked up and believed the other to be at fault. The supervising teacher was bemused – after all, she had seen or heard nothing during the lesson to indicate any problems and was puzzled as to the cause and nature of the argument.

After much investigation it appeared that these laptop computers, this manna from heaven, these great devices to help these students survive the school environment were, in fact, through some infra-red laser system, capable of communicating with each other across the room. The two students had been conducting a technological argument right under the teacher's nose.

Further strategies for Detached students include:

- Teach basic study skills (e.g. reading for the main idea, note taking, outlining, highlighting, estimation, problem solving).

- Make the subject more meaningful to the student by relating the subject matter to the student's environment, using the student's name frequently.

- Follow a less desirable task with a more desirable task making the completion of the first a prerequisite before the second.

- Assign a peer tutor to work with the student.

- Break down large tasks into smaller tasks.

- Give directions in a variety of ways but make sure the student knows directions will only be given once.

- Use a variety of high-interest means to communicate with the student (e.g. auditory, visual, manipulatives, etc.).

- Seat the student close to the source of information.

- Provide student with appropriate time limits for assignments.

- Stop at various points to check on the student's attention and comprehension.

- Present directions following the outline: What; How; Materials; When.

Finally

The story about Alfie does not, unfortunately, have a totally happy ending, at least from the school's point of view. This was partly due to Alfie's home situation, which meant that he attended the school on a part-time basis only, and left before completing his GCSEs. Alfie, on the other hand, would have every right to feel that things had worked out well. The last the school heard he was working for his Dad's very successful software computer company and probably making a lot more money today than all of his former teachers put together.

11
AD/HD with Impulsivity

AD/HD is sometimes very deceptive in the ways it manifests itself. One such case was that of Lucy. She was 5 feet 10 inches tall, 16 years old, with blonde hair, and always dressed fashionably. Many people remarked on her 'stunning' good looks. But Lucy was very unpopular with her peers. One of her teachers recalled one very sad memory of her going to him at the end of the Easter term and asking to borrow a basketball for the holidays. This was really a strange request, as Lucy was not known to have any particular enthusiasm for basketball when she was required to play the game at school. When pressed on the matter she admitted that it was to give her something to do during the break, as nobody wanted to spend time with her during the next two weeks. 'They all think I'm silly,' she explained, still maintaining that degree of optimism only she could offer in such circumstances. The thing was that although he felt sorry for her, her teacher understood exactly what the girl was talking about.

Hyperactivity/Impulsiveness, Clumsiness and Over-talkativeness

Lucy had the unique ability of leaving unintended mayhem in her wake. An example of this would be at the end of the lesson; she would pack up her overflowing book bag, toss her hair backwards and swing the bag over her shoulder in one movement. At this point utter chaos could occur as all personnel and objects within a radius of 6 feet were in serious danger of being struck by both bag and flying books. The more other people (including the teacher) called to her to take care, the more she spun around and more havoc she created. This may sound humorous, and maybe it was at first. But the joke soon wore thin (like most jokes do) when it went on for too long. People began to think: 'This happens too often to be funny.'

Lucy's hyperactivity and impulsivity not only involved this form of motor clumsiness, but it had a verbal aspect too. Lucy seemed to have enormous difficulty in stopping herself from saying whatever happened to be in her mind at the time. Again, what seemed at first like charming, youthful exuberance soon became tiresome and irritating as Lucy simply talked and talked and talked. This was another reason for her peers to avoid her. It was heart-rending for staff to see Lucy's fellow students avoiding her during breaktimes, and being unwilling to sit near her in class. But staff too had to admit to finding her exasperating.

Being with Lucy sometimes felt like being overwhelmed by something inescapable. Lucy monopolised people: craving their attention through a constant stream of chatter and questions. No matter how much attention she was given, it never seemed enough. The subtle and not so subtle cues that most people notice when the person they are talking to has had enough (e.g. looking away, ceasing to respond, turning away, sighing) seemed to make no impression on Lucy at all. Lucy's talkativeness was not simply a minor irritation, it was a major source of difficulty for her in that it made the forming of friendships virtually impossible.

In some circumstances the consequences were potentially even worse. In confined situations, such as on one long coach trip to Switzerland, Lucy found herself threatened with violence by fellow students, and having to be protected by staff. A 26-hour journey is enough to place anyone under stress. Stress in turn erodes tolerance levels. On this occasion the staff too were finding it difficult to maintain their habitually calm manner in dealing with Lucy. As the journey went on, and as the holiday unfolded, it became clear that Lucy, partly for her own protection, was to spend most of her time attached like velcro to a staff member. With staff, Lucy's chatter usually took the form of an incessant stream of questions:

'Mr O'Regan, what time do we get to the slopes?'

'Does my hair look OK?'

'What time is lunch?'

'Do you think the boys from the other school like me?'

'Why? What? When? How? Where? . . .'

All of this would continue regardless of the staff member's state. Whether they were reading, trying to sleep on the coach, talking to someone else, calculating the exchange rate, or listening attentively to Lucy, it was all the same to her.

In the classroom these same problems interfered with the learning and teaching processes in predictable ways. Lucy seemed almost never capable of settling to a pattern of study, but rather constantly commandeered the attention of others with her chatter and questions.

The potentially darker consequences of this kind of impulsiveness is illustrated by another incident involving Lucy. One day when walking back from the school sports field Lucy picked up a long, quite heavy stick and after a few minutes of scraping it along a wall tossed it over the wall, where it landed on a woman who was watering plants in her garden. The red-faced lady proceeded to storm out of her house and demanded to know who was the culprit.

'It was me,' Lucy said innocently, and without hesitation.

The injured party was taken aback by the prompt admission, but was not satisfied with this. An angry telling off followed in which Lucy was eventually reduced to tears. School staff had to intervene to resolve the situation. It had taken time for Lucy to connect her careless action with the possibility that she might have injured someone.

Strategies

In order to establish some degree of order into her life and that of others in the school the following strategies were used:

1. A structured framework was established at home and school by setting up a Study Skills chart brought to class daily. This chart listed the basic skills required (planning, reviewing, sequencing, summarising, etc.), and she was required to keep a record of her use of these skills in each lesson.

2. Parents were directly involved in the setting up of a structured programme, and bi-weekly parent meetings were held for the first two months then monthly for three more months.

3. After consultation with the school's medical adviser (a consultant child psychiatrist), medication was prescribed to improve her impulse control and thus enable her to be trained in organisational skills.

4. Lucy was recruited to act as a Teacher Assistant in helping younger pupils. This was designed to reinforce her self-esteem in positive socialisation experiences, as well as her need to feel responsibility for others.

5. Lucy was also encouraged and given support to develop an interest in more individualised activities such as swimming, biking and martial arts.

It is often the case that students who experience difficulties in relating to their immediate peers get on better with older and younger people. As a result staff in Lucy's school found that using an older student to help in one of the Lower School classes often provides much mutual benefit. Staff were initially worried that the older, impulsive/hyperactive student would be a disruptive influence, but found that this was not the case.

Lucy, who was pretty much shunned by her peers, proved to be quite brilliant as a Lower School assistant. The younger students responded well to her gregarious nature, creativity and energy, and Lucy found this to be a setting where she could be well-ordered and structured in her approach. This may not be as remarkable an outcome as it might at first seem. For in helping the younger students to develop self-organisation skills (skills which Lucy herself had difficulty acquiring) Lucy was reinforcing and developing her own skills in this area. The younger students and her interaction with them provided the concrete learning experience that students with AD/HD often need in order to thrive.

General strategies for students who are hyperactive and impulsive include:

*   Maintain supervision at all times and in all areas of the school environment.

*   Be mobile to be near the student.

*   Explain to the student that he/she should be satisfied with personal best rather than expecting perfection.

*   Assist the student at the beginning of each task to reduce impulsive responses.

*   Make the student aware of the reasons we must practise responsibility (others' rights, property not damaged).

*   Deliver a predetermined signal (hand or verbal cue) once the student begins to exhibit impulsive behaviour.

*   Make sure the student does not become involved in over-stimulating activities in the playground during PE, breaktimes and lunchtimes (etc.). Structure this time.

- Make sure the student understands which areas in the classroom are off limits to them.

- Try to avoid leaving students in unstructured situations, except for very specific and well-thought-out reasons, and always with supervision.

- Maintain regular and positive communication with parents.

Finally

Lucy is now enjoying a successful career as a kindergarten teacher.

12
AD/HD with Obsessions

One beautiful hot summer's morning an enthusiastic teacher said to her Key Stage 2 class: 'Isn't this a beautiful day! It's so good to be alive!'

'Except for dogs,' said Jack, morosely.

'Dogs?' the teacher asked, puzzled and somewhat irritated at having been interrupted, and in such a deflating way.

'Yes, dogs,' said Jack. 'Don't you know that a lot of people leave them locked in cars, especially on hot sunny days, and they can get very ill that way.'

This was typical of Jack. His view of the world was really very distinctive, and seldom shared by those around him. And in spite of his morose responses on those occasions, he always seemed at his happiest when he was in that world of his. For Jack the subject of animals was his central preoccupation. No matter what the subject in hand was Jack would be drawn to making a connection between it and animals; no matter how convoluted, tenuous, or plain bizarre the connection was. Unfortunately, it was very hard to interest him in anything which for him did not relate to animals. This made communicating with Jack difficult. Teachers, his parent and peers could never be sure that they were on the same 'wavelength' as Jack. They might think they were having a conversation with him about the weather, but Jack's half of the conversation was about animals. In fact so long as Jack was able to indulge his obsession with animals he did not appear to be interested in communicating with others – unless the communication was to do with animals.

Obsession and the Power of Reframing

The social implications of this were illustrated when Jack was taken with class-mates on a trip to London Zoo. His excitement at the prospect was almost tangible. For weeks leading up to this trip Jack plagued his teachers with the question: 'How long will it be until the trip to the Zoo?' On the day of the event Jack and the rest of the group arrived at the zoo where they were introduced to Mr Taylor. He proved to be an excellent guide (and just what the Head of the school had asked for): patient, understanding, and able to connect with a group of students some of whom could be very difficult to get on with. Of all of them, however, it was with Jack that Mr Taylor seemed to have the most obvious rapport. Throughout the day Jack was never further than a matter of inches from Mr Taylor's side, listening intently and offering his own well-grounded impressions and thoughts on the various exhibits. A wonderful time was had by all, especially Jack, who must have thought he had died and gone to heaven when they reached the reptile house, since of all the animal kingdom, snakes were his real passion.

After the tour was over the students met in a lecture theatre for a short final talk from Mr Taylor, at the end of which he asked for questions from the students about the day's visit. After a couple of seconds up popped Jack's hand and Mr Taylor beamed with pleasure at the star pupil – his new friend.

'So then, Jack, what is your question?'

'How much do you earn?' asked Jack.

As the titters and sniggers from the other students started, the teachers' faces reddened and Mr Taylor appeared crushed and disappointed at what was widely seen as Jack's cheek. It seemed all the worse because of the rapport that had seemed to grow between Mr Taylor and Jack. Had Jack really been conning everyone, including Mr Taylor, the whole day? Was this his way of asserting the superiority of his own encyclopaedic knowledge of animals over that of a mere zoo guide? Jack was not above this kind of behaviour, especially when he had an audience. Playing the class clown was one of the ways he compensated for his conspicuously poor classroom performance. And so this excellent day ended on a discordant note, with the teacher in charge apologising to Mr Taylor, scolding Jack for his rudeness, before unceremoniously marching the students back to school. This kind of disappointment is something that people who work with students with social and behavioural difficulties get used to. What made it worse was the fact that Mr Taylor, an innocent bystander, had been embarrassed in this way.

In retrospect one of the staff members who accompanied this trip has come to reframe Jack's apparent impertinence. It was just possible that for once maybe Jack wasn't trying to be the class clown but perhaps he really did want to know how much Mr Taylor earned in order to determine whether or not this could be a job that he might want to do in the future. This doesn't mean that Jack's question was any less impertinent. What it might mean, however, is that the impertinence was unintended. A way of salvaging the situation might have been for one of the teachers to intervene when Jack asked the question, to refine the enquiry to one about the nature of Mr Taylor's job and how a young person might go about getting such a job. Jack's obsessive interest in animals made all else of secondary importance, even the feelings of someone with whom he had made such a warm association.

The Dangerous Side of Obsession

It was not just at school that Jack appeared to have his own agenda but many other stories concern his interactions in the home environment. One of these concerns 'Jasper's Flight'.

Jasper so it seems was a rather overweight and very sedentary tabby cat who belonged to the family. In addition to animals Jack, apparently, was very fond of toy soldiers and was especially impressed with a recently purchased parachute kit with which he was able to propel his Combat GI out of his bedroom window and into the garden below. Perhaps this was another case of Jack making a connection with his passion for animals. Whatever the reason it was not long before Jasper was being prepared for his first parachute drop – out of a third-floor window. Being quite scientific in his planning Jack weighed Jasper and carried out a test drop, using a concrete garden gnome of a weight roughly equivalent to that of Jasper. After the gnome had landed safely in the paddling pool that Jack had placed strategically below in order to absorb the impact, Jasper was strapped into a specially designed harness and chute. As he was lifted towards the window about to begin his journey into the unknown Jasper suddenly realized the extent of his predicament and began to struggle, and he embarked upon his descent with a front paw caught up in the cords of one side of the chute. As a result the chute only partially inflated.

Fortunately for Jasper all of this additional movement had taken him slightly off the preordained flight path and instead of hitting the water, with rather more force than anticipated he bounced off the side of the air-filled paddling pool. He was last seen sprinting into the nearest hedge with his harness and chute wrapped about him, apparently none the worse for wear, but with a new-found mistrust for the human race.

It may seem surprising to some people that a boy like Jack, with his passion for animals, could put a cat in such danger. But this would be to misunderstand the nature of obsession. For children like Jack their interest in animals may be of a highly technical nature: to do with the animals' physical characteristics and dimensions, their speed, their patterns of eating, habitat and so on. In short, their interest in animals may be an interest in the animal as an object rather than as a living, feeling being.

Social Effects of Obsessive Behaviour

Students with obsessions are very difficult to relate to on a social basis. Their tendency to inhabit their own peculiar worlds, and their strange way of relating to the outside world make them appear unrewarding and even threatening to their peers. Sometimes this can lead to the child becoming the victim of bullying. In Jack's case, however, there was a tendency for Jack's school peers to leave Jack alone, and to avoid interacting with him.

One unexpected by-product of this social isolation was Jack's tendency, whenever he encountered new situations, to act as though they were undiscovered by others. After all, his lack of communication with others meant that he had little or no concept of what others were thinking, or of the general pool of 'common knowledge' that most of us take for granted. This was illustrated one very cold day, when he was part of a group making a field trip to Hampton Court. After a fairly uneventful visit to the main building the students were allowed to walk outside into the gardens, although for obvious reasons we avoided the maze. Finally, when staff and students gathered together at the collection point it was noted that Jack was missing. The first thing the leader of the trip did was to scold the student who had been assigned to stay with Jack. But even the teacher could not help sympathising with the boy's complaint that 'Jack always wanders off – he doesn't take any notice of anybody!'

Eventually Jack was found. The scene was bizarre. Jack, in a trance-like state, was blowing out thick waves of condensed air in the direction of a very frightened elderly woman, who appeared in great distress as she stood against a wall, apparently transfixed to the spot. Jack was simply displaying his new magical discovery. Further to this he appeared content to repeat the process for however long it took until positive recognition of his invention would be forthcoming.

It took a while to reassure the woman that there was really nothing to be afraid of. Jack was persuaded to apologise after a period of debriefing and subsequently wrote a further letter to express how sorry he was that she had misunderstood his intentions and that he had upset her.

Hypersensitivity

In addition to these sometimes disturbing behaviours, Jack also exhibited a range of extreme sensitivities. Jack found changing for sports activities in group changing rooms very distressing. He was also extremely fussy about his possessions and became very upset when he thought that these had been interfered with by others, or when what he saw as his private space (such as his desk or locker) was invaded.

One last example shows how sensitive staff should be in their handling of a student like Jack. The incident occurred during an end-of-year staff pantomime of Cinderella to which all the students were invited. During the performance the scene called for an Ugly Sister to flirt with a male student in the audience. The male member of staff playing the sister, part blinded by his extravagant wig made the mistake of choosing a student on the first row which in this case happened to be Jack. As the audience laughed a look of sheer horror came over Jack's face at what he saw as his total humiliation and he pulled up the hood of his jacket in order to hide himself from everyone. He remained in this state throughout the duration of the performance and until he left the school that day.

Strategies

Over the years main strategies for Jack included:

1. Providing Jack with a specific seating placement in class, making sure all students understood this was his area, and Jack's need to have his territory respected by others.

2. Special measures were introduced to support Jack during changes to schedule and routines of the school day.

3. Counselling was provided to help Jack improve his communication and self-help skills.

4. Providing him with a private place in which to change clothing for PE/sports.

5. Not forcing him to be involved in activities which appeared to make him feel uncomfortable.

6. Specific careers counselling for future school transition.

Additional interventions for the obsessional type include:

- Make certain student has enough time to perform activities.

- If necessary allow the student to practise something new in private before doing it in front of others.

- If a student is uncomfortable at school allow a parent or relative to stay with the student all day if necessary. Gradually reduce the time the person remains with the student.

- Provide a schedule by which the student gradually increases the length of time spent at school each day or on a particular activity.

- Avoid negative criticism of the student.

- Identify a peer who readily engages in social activities to act as a model for the student.

- Make sure distracting sounds (e.g. talking, movement noises, bells, etc.) are all silenced when directions are being given to the student.

- Stand directly in front of the student when delivering information.

- Use pictures, diagrams, chalkboard and gestures when delivering information.

- Provide positive reinforcement to the student for directing and maintaining attention to important sounds in the environment.

- Do not use over-elaborate language when talking to the student. Short sharp statements tend to be more effective.

Finally

Jack finally achieved a clutch of good passes at GCSE and left school. Over time there was a steady improvement in his self-regulatory behaviour, though his core difficulties still persist to some degree. He is still interested in animals and hopes to take up a career in this area.

13
AD/HD with Learning Difficulties

Ruby had a wide range of learning difficulties, including auditory processing problems and literacy difficulties, coupled with a tendency for organisational problems, avoidance and procrastination. Homework assignments and sports kit were the main problems with this student. She would forget to bring in both on regular occasions despite warnings, punishments and all the positive reinforcement mechanisms known to the school staff.

Organisation Problems

Discussions between school staff, Ruby and her parents were inconclusive, until one day, in frustration, Ruby broke down and sobbed: 'It's just too much to do altogether!' It transpired that Ruby simply did not want to carry two bags to school. Her solution to not having a single bag big enough to accommodate all she needed to take to school had been to compromise by taking some homework, certain items of her sports kit and part of her lunch, as long as it would all fit in the same single bag. The solution to the school's problem only arrived when Ruby received a birthday gift of a bigger school bag from her Grandmother.

Ruby was infamous in school for her laconic attitude to life and was known for her alternative views on many subjects and in particular the issue of timekeeping. One of her stock answers was that 'The problem with my parents is that they make me go to bed in the evening when I am not tired and then they get me up in the morning when I am tired!'

It was not just the problems of getting her up, dressed and out to school in this particular case. Ruby had a habit of literally falling asleep on the train on her way to school. This happened on at least five different occasions and what should have been a 40-minute train journey became a 3-hour round trip. To prevent this happening again Ruby was provided with an alarm watch, checked by her parents every morning that would activate one station before her stop. This appeared to work well.

The Power of Positive Reinforcement

The encouragement of desired behaviours through the use of positive reinforcement strategies is well known as an effective form of intervention for children with AD/HD. It is always a good idea for teachers to inquire of parents and the child him- or herself of their experience of positive reinforcement, simply to find out what works and what doesn't for an individual student. In Ruby's case her experience of positive reinforcement had not been at all successful. In her previous school – which had been run by a religious order – the reinforcement system had relied largely on cards containing a variety of religious images that had been given to students for exceptional performance in academic and behavioural terms. The system seems to have been unsuccessful, for Ruby at least, because it failed to fulfil the principle of short-term rewards. In this case the students were told that the more cards they received the easier it would be for them to get into heaven! The promise of a happy eternity was not a meaningful incentive to a student who found it difficult to think as far ahead as the end of the day.

Over time Ruby showed very good progress. Through specific teaching and training focused on her difficulties in reading, spelling and maths measurable improvements were achieved, and her confidence and self-esteem improved too. In terms of study skills however improvement was a less linear matter, and although all of the standard techniques were tried it was a constant and consistent battle to have her remember to bring what she needed when she needed it, and to hand assignments in on time. Her apparently laissez-faire approach tended to stretch patience. Eventually, however, it was Ruby herself who found a wonderful way of helping her teaching staff to help her.

The Power of Listening to the Student

It all started in a routine way when at the end of a lesson once again Ruby said she had left her homework sheet in her locker. She would hand it in at the beginning of lunchtime. The teacher did not want to wait. An altercation occurred during which Ruby said: 'There is more than one way to Dominic's house, Sir!' When he asked her to explain what she meant Ruby replied that she would tell him at lunchtime. Intrigued, the teacher relented. Good as her word Ruby returned with the homework at lunchtime and told the following story.

It seemed disorganisation was a trait of Ruby's family. Her Dad was often unable to find his way when reading a map during a family car outing, or when delivering Ruby or her younger brother to children's parties. What should have been 2-mile journeys could become 7-, 8- or 9-mile tours of the local countryside. At times this led Ruby's mother to lose her temper with her husband, and arguments often ensued in the car, with Ruby and her brother Ben being caught in the crossfire. At the end of one such extended journey, as they pulled into the driveway the mother was continuing to complain when suddenly 4-year-old Ben called out: 'Stop it! Stop fighting! It really doesn't matter if we're a bit wrong does it? We got here didn't we?'

After a stunned silence Ben then added determinedly, 'After all there's more than one way to Dominic's house!'

This story was important for a number of reasons. First, at the surface level it told an important truth. After all, getting to the right destination is often more important than the route you take. When we are feeling generous, the first thing we often say to late visitors or dinner guests is, 'Don't worry about being late, we are just glad that you got here!' Second, the fact that Ruby was able to use the story in this situation showed that she was prepared to really think about her apparent problem. And in this case she was right to make the point that actually there was no real problem. What she had done in fact was to reframe the problem that the teacher attributed to Ruby's forgetfulness as a problem of the teacher's unnecessary rigidity. This was important for Ruby's sense of self-esteem and her capacity for reflection and self-regulation. Third, this interaction between the teacher and Ruby was important in itself. The teacher might have responded to Ruby's story as a very cheeky challenge to his authority, and have punished her accordingly. After all, the story was used as a justification for not carrying out the teacher's initial instruction. The fact that the teacher was prepared to give Ruby the benefit of the doubt and hear her out was an important act of trust. Trust is essential to the teacher–student relationship. We learn to trust ourselves only after we have experienced the trust of others, and self-trust is an essential component of self-regulation. This was truly a case where the teacher learned something from the student, and, to his credit, treated the knowledge as valuable.

Strategies

Overall for Ruby the key strategies used were as follows:

1. To make sure that teaching was multi-sensory and individualised.

2. Provide extra reinforcement for extension reading skills in English, Maths, Science.

3. Specific use of over-teaching techniques, using computer software.

4. Assignment of a student 'buddy' to help in organisation and mandatory attendance in homework club.

5. Specific training in study skills and exam revision.

6. Counselling and medication options used in multi-disciplinary approach.

Due to the nature of Ruby's difficulties she was able to qualify for a whole set of special arrangements at the GCSE exams. These included 25% extra time and the use of a scribe and reader (except in English Language) to write down her answers and help in comprehension of the questions. She also qualified for the use of a computer to type out responses and even the use of a prompter in case she drifted off into an unrelated dream world in the exam.

Other ideas:

- Provide reinforcement for the student for demonstrating comprehension of reading material.

- Reduce distracting stimuli around the student to help them concentrate on reading/task assignments.

- Provide the student with a written 1-, 2- and 3-step structure for performing specific activities.

- Have the student maintain a sight word vocabulary approach in order to teach key words and phrases and reinforce dictionary skills.

- Have the student present test questions based on previous information.

- Provide the student with a list of necessary materials for the day.

- Remind the student at the end of the day to prepare a specific set of materials for next day.

- Make sure all personal property is labelled with the student's name.

- Consider the student's work space and where appropriate provide a larger or otherwise more suitable work space.

- Require any assignments not correctly done for any reason to be redone.

- Evaluate the appropriateness of the task to determine: (1) if the task is too difficult (2) the appropriate time allocation for the task.

Finally

English despite Ruby's dyslexia was an area of strength for her, along with drama, and after leaving school she gained a place at a drama school, with the ambition of becoming a professional actress.

14
AD/HD with High Ability

Most well-informed and experienced teachers would agree that being flexible and willing to meet students halfway are essential qualities for working successfully with difficult students. Because most students are compliant with school rules, and readily acquiesce to teacher authority, however, it sometimes difficult for teachers to deal with the student who also seeks to assert power, and to be acknowledged as being powerful. David was one such student, who combined a keen intellect and well-developed academic abilities with a clear sense of his own power, especially in situations where he was being required to submit unconditionally to the power of others.

Giving Power and Getting Co-operation

When 14-year-old David first arrived at the school he would always seem to lose his pen or avoid taking it to his classes, although he had all his books and other materials. This would annoy the teachers greatly, often getting lessons off to a bad start. As a result over the subsequent weeks teachers tried many positive and negative reinforcement mechanisms that they knew, but still he did not bring a pen to class.

One day at the start of a lesson after the daily 5 or 6 minutes of 'Where is your pen today David?' both student and teacher frustrations were at boiling point, when David asked: 'Well, why don't you keep a pen here for me?'

The teacher's initial reaction was a refusal to comply with the request. The teacher was concerned that to concede on this point would undermine her authority. This was in spite of the fact that she secretly acknowledged to herself that it really wasn't a bad idea and wished that she had thought of it first. Swallowing her pride, she decided that a good idea was a good idea. Over the next few weeks she kept David's pen in her desk and gave it to him at the start of the lesson and he returned it to her at the end. Then one day David brought a pen with him. After that he never needed the teacher's assistance in this matter again.

It seems that for David the weight of rules and expectations that his new school was imposing on him was becoming intolerable. The pen had been 'a bridge too far'. David needed to retain some sense of control and to have that acknowledged by staff. He was also very stubborn.

An example of this was an incident relayed by his parents. They had asked him to tidy his room one Friday night. This had been an area of contention for some weeks and with the instruction that he wasn't to come downstairs until this was done. David refused to comply and the lines of battle were drawn. The weekend came and went. He next surfaced on the Monday morning in order to go back to school, the room remaining in disarray.

Having said this, he was a manageable boy on most occasions except when something triggered his deep seam of obstinacy. When this occurred no matter what the outcome David remained determined to wage a war of attrition for however long it took. At school the issue involved homework. Despite being a fairly compliant student in class he truly loathed homework and basically refused to do it whatever the consequences.

After weeks of disciplining him for his failure to produce the required work, and despite serious pressure from teachers, parents, counsellors and even peers, still no homework would be completed. One morning however, David arrived at school early and asked to see the head teacher. The Head explained that he would have to wait in one of the classrooms while he attended to another matter. But before he left the Head watched David carefully take out of his bag the hated homework assignments and start to write.

'What are you doing, David?' asked the bemused Headmaster.

'Schoolwork,' he replied quietly and simply. Without looking up he continued writing.

After this David came to school early every day, on his own initiative, to do his homework. And in this area at least peace reigned.

Subversion

It was easy to feel frustrated with David. He was a very bright boy, capable of outstanding work, but erratic in his performance. All too often, it seemed, he preferred to direct his unquestionable ability to subversion rather than work. He was one of those students who always had too much to say both in terms of pushing the behavioural boundaries or simply complaining. For example, some of his complaints included:

> 'Why do we have to change rooms so often? Why don't you teachers move? My Dad works in an office and has a desk in the same place that he sits at all day, and it works well for him. If I had that same opportunity don't you think I'd be more productive?'

> On the subject of breaktimes: 'It's beyond belief that you teachers send us outside during our own free time in all weather, whether we want to go or not. You are basically encouraging us all to take up smoking!'

> 'You can't make me do this work!'

> 'I don't care if you do put me in detention I'm not going to do it anyway!'

Such challenges can be very wearing for teachers, and lead them to simply give up on the student who just doesn't want to know. Then, negative responses from the teacher challenge the student to further rebellion and initiate a downward spiral of conflict that ultimately undermines both teacher and student.

Of course, not only did David's antagonism act as a distraction to teachers and his peers, it also acted as a barrier to his learning. It acted as a way of maintaining a distance between David and his teachers which made engaging him in work which he found challenging or not so interesting extremely difficult.

Strategies

Key strategies for David included:

1. Differentiated assignments in a number of classes and for homework.

2. Differentiated classroom schedule.

3. Audio/Video taping of arguments between the teacher/David in order for him to reflect on the impact and timing of his comments in a group situation.

4. Giving David responsibility for helping out with computer networking and solving of both hardware and software problems in the computer room and some other classes.

5. A contract was made between David and the school on specific daily/weekly targets/issues together with parental involvement.

6. Counselling was provided to help David work on further specific issues.

After reviewing the tape we had made one day of a classroom confrontation that had involved him he was genuinely surprised and a little shocked at the way in which he behaved.
Additional strategies include:

• Have the student keep a chart or graph representing the number of tasks completed at school and at home.

• Assign the student shorter tasks for homework (e.g. out of twenty problems set for maths homework only have five to be completed at first). Gradually increase number required.

• Encourage the student to ask for clarification of classroom assignments.

• Interact frequently with the student to maintain involvement with class assignments.

• Explain to the student that work not completed during work time will need to done during other times.

• Take steps to deal with student refusal to perform an assignment. Send to time-out area, etc. Avoid engaging in argument on these occasions.

• Maintain consistency in daily routine.

• Communicate clearly when assignment needs to be completed and structure time limits.

- Provide alternatives for both format of directions and also completion of work using tape-recorders, laptop computers, etc.

- Make it acceptable and positive for the student to ask questions about what he or she does not understand or has concerns about.

- Have a box at the front table for the student to write down questions or comments that you can reply to later.

Finally

In addition to the measures described above, a key aim with David was to establish a positive relationship between him and his teachers. Staff found quite quickly that although he knew how to annoy, argue and confront he didn't know how to respond to a teacher being positive about him, especially if the teacher rang David's parent or wrote a positive note home. As time passed and David began to trust the goodwill of his teachers, he began to volunteer to do things around the school such as help out in the computer lab. This was a major breakthrough as he had rejected early attempts to involve him in this way. Through his expertise in this area David networked four new computers and saved £300 for the school that would otherwise have been spent on getting in an outside consultant.

15
AD/HD with Conduct Disorder

The child who exhibits AD/HD together with serious conduct problems poses challenges to the teacher on all fronts. Students with this combination of problems will have some or all of the problems of overactivity, impulsiveness and inattentiveness coupled with a negative attitude and very challenging behaviour. Conduct disorder is characterised by a severe tendency to break rules, defy the teacher's authority, and disrupt lessons. Anti-social behaviour, including stealing and aggression to others are also aspects of conduct disorder. These features are often (though not always) accompanied by a very poor attitude to school-work. As with other cases that we have discussed, the behavioural and attitudinal problems can mask the learning problems associated with AD/HD and sometimes cause teachers to misinterpret them as being the product of the student's attitude. A distinctive feature of the child with conduct disorder, however, is the intensity and frequency of their disruptive behaviour. Also, where many of the behavioural patterns we have discussed in relation to other students can be a cause of weariness and irritation to their peers and teachers, conduct disorder is defined by its effect of inspiring fear and a sense of danger in those exposed to it. Tom was one such student.

Although Tom was only 14 when he arrived at the school, he had already been a student at five previous schools. Although the precise details of why he had moved so frequently were difficult to establish, it soon became clear that he did not have very positive expectations of his new school. He presented himself as someone with very little interest in school and less interest in working co-operatively with staff. He also showed that he could be aggressive and provocative towards some of his fellow students, whilst at the same time seeking to ally himself with others.

Searching for Patterns and Finding Solutions

Tom was a complex individual who was often disruptive, but not always when one would expect. In dealing with him over the early months staff noticed that more often than not the sparks would fly due to seemingly insignificant issues. He would sometimes fly into frightening, uncontrollable rages for no other apparent reason than perhaps his pencil lead had broken, or a fellow student walking too close to his desk had brushed against his arm, or in response to an innocent remark. Whereas the more obvious triggers such as issues around classroom rules or homework completion were less likely to set him off. As a result, the staff efforts to enhance Tom's self-esteem, through praise for work produced and for his general compliance with major school and class rules, tended to be undermined when Tom would appear regularly in detention or on report for his behaviour.

Usually in such cases one or two common features can be identified as the major factors which act as triggers for negative behaviour, such as a particular recurring event, specific teacher–student relationship or a particular topic or class grouping. With this in mind attempts were made by staff to analyse the factors that might be causing the problems (see Chapter 6 for observational and recording techniques). There was no obvious pattern to the apparent triggering events (e.g. the pencil lead breaking), or in the locations (i.e. time of day; subject; teacher), or in the way that the behaviours were handled by staff. What did become clear, however, was that there would be bad days and good days. On good days there would be no problems, on the same day in the next week, however, there could be Tom-initiated mayhem in every lesson. The question then was: if there is no obvious cause in the school environment for Tom's behaviour, is there something about Tom that is different on these occasions that may be the trigger? Staff were asked to consider this question carefully and report any observations that came from this. After not too long it was discovered that these tantrum days coincided with the absence of his baseball hat. It transpired that he was so concerned about the appearance of his hair, that he became extremely upset when he did not have his baseball cap to hide his haircut.

Staff soon found that by keeping a spare baseball hat at school for Tom to use on those days when he forgot or could not find his own (common problems for children with AD/HD), it was possible to reduce the frequency of his 'trivial' tantrums. Concerns by some staff that this concession might be seen as tantamount to condoning Tom's negative behaviour would seem to have been unfounded. If we look at it from Tom's viewpoint it is very likely that he welcomed the substitute hat as a relief from the distress that had been the underlying trigger for the tantrums. This points to the way in which this intervention helped to make everyone's life a lot easier, freeing teachers to teach and students to learn. There remained, of course, the problem of Tom's way of reacting to distress, but this was not going to be helped by continuing to expose him to unnecessary distress in the classroom.

A similar problem concerned Tom's tendency to remove his shoes in class, complaining that 'They're too uncomfortable,' or 'I can't concentrate with these on.' This was remedied quite easily by providing some old pairs of the staff members' house slippers which could be used by any student, including Tom, if they felt their shoes were uncomfortable to the point of distraction in class. This was a carefully judged intervention that took into account the difference between what was seen as an issue of genuine distress (i.e. the hair sensitivity), and this more self-indulgent matter. In this case Tom had to understand that although removing his shoes might relieve his discomfort, it might be at the expense of others' comfort (in the olfactory sense). The solution, therefore, was designed to show Tom that whilst his needs were being taken seriously, so too were those of his peers. Also, the choice of a relatively unattractive alternative form of footwear (i.e. 'granddad slippers') meant that students, including Tom, would only opt for these if they felt genuine discomfort.

Stealing and Other Anti-Social Behaviours

A more serious problem was Tom's stealing, both in and out of school. The real difficulty faced by the school here was how to handle the problem. Clearly, there are fairly universal attitudes to theft, which usually lead to punishment of one kind or another. These attitudes, however, tend to be based in the idea that theft is an act of premeditation and choice. The school, however, was faced with the complicating possibility that Tom's thieving might be a by-product of his AD/HD and an act of impulsivity rather than premeditation. The crucial difference is that one is an act outside the individual's conscious control whilst the other is very much based on conscious choice. This had important consequences for the way in which the school would handle the issue. On examination, it was found that Tom engaged in examples of both.

One of the key means of discriminating between these forms of stealing was the post-incident interview. Sometimes, during these interviews, Tom tried to cover his tracks and indicated that he had already worked out a strategy to block the staff investigation. At these times, holes would soon begin to appear in the logic of the story, and as the story broke down he would become increasingly defensive, attempting to plant responsibility onto others. On other occasions, however, Tom provided no story, and seemed genuinely bewildered about the incident, offering no explanation, not even a defence.

Clearly, there is always the danger that a student might learn to play-act the bewildered impulsive to avoid punishment. Staff have to use their knowledge of individuals to make judgements about this. In Tom's case acts of theft which were detected were always dealt with first in terms of having the stolen property returned or other reparation. Also, parents were informed. If the theft were seen as a premeditated act then the immediate focus of staff intervention would be to help Tom appreciate the practical, personal and ethical consequences of the act. This might also involve punishment as an illustration of consequences. Where the problem was seen to be an impulsive act, then in addition to these measures a focus would also be placed on Tom's strategies and techniques for impulse control, with the moral and practical aspects being highlighted as aids to impulse control. If anything the intervention for the impulsive act was the more time-consuming and gruelling for Tom.

In addition to stealing, Tom had three particularly anti-social behaviours which he directed against peers. The first was to try to trip up students as they walked past him. The second involved cussing students under his breadth during class. Both of these on more than one occasion had resulted in a great deal of fallout including punishments and parent conferences which really achieved minimal impact. Third, he seemed to have the knack of knowing exactly which emotional buttons to press in order to make certain members of staff lose their tempers, and seemed to take pleasure in this.

Strategies

The main strategies with Tom were as follows:

1. Training staff in how to depersonalise situations.
2. Use of video to show Tom how he responded in group situations.

3. Supervision of Tom during changeover and breaktime/lunchtime situations through use of a student buddy/classroom assistant.

4. Contracts were established, using Tom's input together with teacher/parent input.

5. Getting Tom to act as a teacher assistant student in the Middle School group to tutor maths and the school talent show.

6. Specific medical and counselling strategies to deal with impulsivity, oppositionality and anger management.

7. Tom's parents were encouraged to spend time in the classroom during lessons, and were asked to attend on field trips with Tom.

The Staff–Student Relationship

One of the major battles faced on Tom's behalf was not actually with Tom himself but with some of the teachers who taught him. At worst they would be resigned to the fact that in every class he was going to cause trouble and, as labelling theory tells us, Tom lived down to theory expectations.

When confronted with a teacher who, after yet another disruptive incident involving Tom, wanted him suspended, the Headteacher hit on a novel intervention. First, he asked the teacher, who knew Tom well, why he thought he never had any success with Tom.

'He's just a bad un,' he said.

Then the Head asked the teacher to write a short account that evening, in which he took Tom's viewpoint and described his home life, his feelings as a student and attitude towards the school. If the teacher did this, the Head promised, then they would review the suspension request. After all, the Head argued, if Tom gets suspended from this school with his history it could really mean the end of his educational career. This exercise, which would take maybe 30 or 40 minutes was not a lot to ask in these circumstances. Tom was also given an assignment to complete that evening in which he was to take the role of the teacher, and describe what working with Tom was like and how it made him feel.

The next day the teacher and Head met again. To say the teacher's attitude towards Tom had completely changed on the basis of this exercise would be an overstatement, but his written account really did show that he no longer believed Tom to be a 'bad un'. There was a clear recognition that his circumstances were not helpful towards preparation for school and that this probably contributed to his behaviour at school. What had the most powerful effect on the teacher was Tom's assignment. It was full of empathy and insight into the difficulties experienced by teachers of difficult students, containing the line: 'I could never teach me, I don't know why he bothers.' The teacher was greatly moved by this and, although not overnight, a good relationship between the two was established.

Other strategies include:

*   Provide reinforcement for the student for demonstrating appropriate behaviour.

*   Remove student from group activity until he/she can demonstrate appropriate behaviour and self-control.

*   Close supervision in and around the school environment.

- Prevent the student from being overstimulated by an activity in games, breaks, etc.

- Provide the student with a clearly identified list of consequences for inappropriate behaviour.

- Teach the student problem-solving skills, e.g. (1) identify the problem, (2) identify goals and objectives, (3) develop strategies, (4) develop a plan of action, and (5) carry out plan.

- Prevent peers from engaging in those behaviours that would cause the student to fail.

- Show an interest in the student in the classroom: consult students.

- Do not inadvertently reinforce the student's inappropriate behaviour by laughing when the student is silly/rude.

- Have the student put themselves in someone else's place ('How would it make you feel if someone called you daft, dumb or stupid?').

- Remember to separate the behaviour from the person. Do not personalise the situation: it is the behaviour we wish to change.

Finally

Tom did not complete his school career in London as his family relocated back to the USA when he was 16.

16
AD/HD:
Combined Type

At 17 years of age and 6 feet tall Donald was a real handful. He presented all the classic symptoms of AD/HD (combined type) to an extreme degree. He seemed only able to concentrate when he was enjoying the task, for example when engaged in a computer game, often art, or an intensive sporting activity, such as basketball or skateboarding. With difficult or boring tasks he showed almost no perseverance, having enormous difficulty getting started and then quickly going off task. Once off task Donald would do whatever seemed to excite his interest, be it using a handy object as an improvised javelin, or setting light to someone's hair (see below). Getting him to change from one task to another, or to tear himself away from an activity he found interesting or fun were extremely difficult and could lead to heated confrontations. When Donald was not engaged in a stimulating activity he appeared restless and fidgety, apparently unable to keep still or settle. At these times he could easily fall to irritating and provoking anyone he came across. He consistently behaved in ways that showed no consideration for the consequences of his actions either for himself or others. He had enormous difficulty in waiting his turn in queues, conversations or games, and would say and do things he later regretted, which, in turn, led to social difficulties.

In school these problems caused severe disruption to classroom life, interfered with Donald's and other students' learning, threatened their safety, and made life very difficult for staff. Away from the structure and routine of school Donald was highly vulnerable to a wide range of physical, moral and legal dangers, and a constant source of worry to his parents.

Talent and Failure Can Go Hand in Hand

Donald joined the school late in his career from a school in America, and he had never previously played soccer. He was, however, a natural athlete and the best choice for goalkeeper in the school soccer team. He could leap like a gazelle and had excellent hand–eye co-ordination. In training sessions he revealed himself to be an excellent shot saver and was able to dominate his penalty area. In fact, he became so adept at plucking opposing team crosses from out of the air it was not long before he became known as 'Donald the Cat'.

The school's first external fixture of the season was against a neighbouring comprehensive school who had by far the stronger of the two teams. As a result it was to be a 'Donald vs. Goliath' affair with the great reliance being placed on Donald as the last line of defence.

Despite all the odds Donald's team started brightly and went one goal up due to a somewhat unorthodox move, that was not so much a tactic as a symptom of Donald's extreme impulsivity: whenever he received the ball he booted it with great force to the opposite end of the field as if it were a live grenade. This would occur whether his own players were ready or not. On one of the occasions when his forwards were ready Donald carried out this manoeuvre. The opposition, not being used to such a fast-paced game, had been caught napping and Donald's side were suddenly, unexpectedly in the lead. The opposition were skilled players, however, and Donald was kept extremely busy, showing enormous agility as he saved shot after shot.

Unfortunately, Donald's heroic moment was to be short-lived. In the space of an hour he was to descend from star of the day to the player who let the side down. It was a high scoring game but the *coup de grace* to Donald's valiant team was delivered in humiliating circumstances. The final quarter of the game had seen Donald's team actually begin to dominate the play, to the extent that it was the opposition goal-keeper's turn to be harassed as the game stood poised at three goals each. Things had gone very quiet at Donald's end of the pitch. However, Donald's performance had been so good throughout the game that when, with time running out, the opposing centre-forward won the ball there was a feeling among the spectating staff and players alike that Donald the Cat would save the game. However as all eyes followed the attacking player, nearing Donald's goal at speed, it became clear that a vital element was missing from the picture. Donald was not in his goal. In fact Donald was not even on the pitch. The opposing centre-forward shot into an empty net. Meanwhile 'the Cat' was spotted in the open space behind the goal retrieving the corner flag-pole which he had been using for javelin practice since his interest in the game had waned.

In some ways this soccer story shows how sport can serve as a microcosm for the nature of AD/HD. Donald possessed exceptional skills as a goalkeeper, although he was untutored in the sport of soccer. However, what might have been a vehicle for achieving success and admiration became another experience of failure and recrimination. This is not to say that Donald could not have become a successful soccer player. But there can be few inhabitants of soccer-playing countries who are unaware of high profile and (for a time at least) extraordinarily talented footballers whose breathtaking skills can be described only in terms of a gift. They possess skills that training alone cannot produce. Their performance is not driven so much by training as what might be termed 'instinct'. Or, to put it another way, these are players who experience rather than control their gift. The reverse side of this coin, however, is impulsivity: the tendency to go with one's feelings rather than making informed choices. There is an extensive roll call of sporting geniuses whose success and downfall could be described in these terms. They are people for whom the thrill and stimulation of the big match brings out the best of their outstanding talent, whilst in the mundane world of the training ground or the low profile match they appear unexceptional. The problem is, of course, that stimulants often lose their power to stimulate. This may be why the ranks of organisations such as Alcoholics Anonymous and Gamblers

Anonymous probably host far more than their fair share of people who are or once were extremely gifted sports-persons. For these people, when they cease to be stimulated by their chosen field (or the field that has chosen them), their need for stimulation leads them either to a quest for further stimulation, (maybe in the form of stimulant drugs or gambling), or to a search for means of suppressing the need for stimulation, through such means as the use of depressant drugs, like tranquillisers and alcohol.

Stimulation at Any Price

Donald was not an alcoholic or drug addict, but at 17 he was out of control. He was hyperactive, impulsive, hypoactive and with a range of secondary features that included gross organisational difficulties. He craved stimulation of all kinds, physical, sensory and chemical, and would go to any means to get this need met, making him antagonistic towards rules and a danger to himself and others. He combined these characteristics with an unwillingness to accept consequences or responsibility for his actions. The following incident illustrates several of these points.

During a Chemistry class one day the teacher detected a strange burning smell in the room. Despite the fact that all the students were using Bunsen burners in an experiment the teacher did not recognise the odour. As she scanned the room she noticed to her horror that the source of the strange burning smell was the smouldering ends of Melanie Smith's hair. Donald, who was sitting directly behind her, was using his Bunsen burner to light the end strands of Melanie's pony-tail. Melanie was oblivious to what was going on. The teacher quickly and calmly approached Donald, took the Bunsen burner from him and switched off the gas tap. Then after ensuring that Melanie's hair was not likely to burst into flames, said to Donald:

'What on earth do you think you are doing?'

Donald replied straight away by reflex, 'It wasn't me, Miss,' before lowering his head and refusing to speak or look the teacher in the eye.

Strategies

The main strategies for Donald were:

1. Heavy emphasis of structure, rules/guidelines reinforcement.

2. Specific extra time allocated with Mentor at the start and especially the end of each day.

3. Mandatory homework completion at school at the end of the school day although structured break-time routine worked into the schedule.

4. Differentiated daily schedule with only specific teachers assigned to work with him and some classes cut from his timetable. Extra classes assigned in computers/art.

5. Medication regime set up and home evening/weekend routine advised with parents.

6. Maximising positive reinforcement by observing his interests in sports, skateboarding, etc.

The Basketball Break: From Rogue to Role Model

Having Donald for two 50-minute periods in a row, in the same classroom at the same time of day, five days a week was always going to be a taxing proposition for teacher and students. The staff soon realised that a special strategy would be needed, and thus the basketball break was born. This quite simply was that in between the classes, if productivity had been good both in the previous day's second lesson, and in the first lesson of the current day, the class was taken to the gym for a 10-minute game. All the students enjoyed this break in the routine. Donald loved it and hated to miss it so much that his performance in both lessons would be highly controlled and he played an active part in encouraging the positive participation of any other student who might jeopardise the privilege. In essence he became both a role model of the productive student and an auxiliary classroom manager for me.

Finally

Although Donald was a real handful in school his most serious problems occurred outside of school, often during the evenings, at weekends and in the holidays. It is not easy for any parents, no matter how well disciplined, structured and proactive they might be, to manage the behaviour of a wayward 17 year old with serious problems of self-control especially when he was out of the house. It would be one of these that led to Donald's downfall when he finally overstepped the line between impulsive behaviour and delinquency once to often and found himself before the courts.

17
And in the End:
Caring for the Carers

As we have noted many times throughout this book students with AD/HD never exist in a vacuum. The school exists as a complex organisation with its own specific ethos and characteristics which may help or hinder the progress of children with AD/HD. Furthermore, the school exists beneath the weight of a wide range of public expectations, government regulations and sometimes conflicting demands for accountability. In turn the students concerned often come from family settings which are experiencing severe stress. Sometimes this is because of the effect of the child's AD/HD and associated difficulties on the family, and sometimes the child's difficulties are exacerbated by family problems, which might include AD/HD. In this final chapter we reflect briefly on some of the human factors in the school and in family situations and consider some of the practical ways in which these might be addressed.

The Teacher's Dilemma

It is appropriate for teachers and other educational workers to see AD/HD very much from an educational perspective, and to be preoccupied with balancing the needs of the child with AD/HD against those of the rest of the school population. This is by no means an easy task. Teachers often feel unfairly torn between competing demands to achieve high academic results for all students, whilst simultaneously being expected to meet a wide range of complex needs, some of which challenge their ability to provide the best educational opportunities to other students.

Teachers who work with students who exhibit social, emotional and behavioural difficulties, such as those associated with AD/HD, are particularly vulnerable in this respect. This is because they are dealing with a group of students who are viewed, at best, ambiguously by the world at large. These are the students that most teachers do not want to teach, whose particular special educational need uniquely places them at permanent risk of being deprived of educational services through exclusion. And yet, against this background of rejection and insecurity, these same teachers are constantly being exhorted to provide these students with experiences of acceptance and security – the very foundations of personal and educational development.

It is not surprising, therefore, that teachers can sometimes become polarised between those who, at one extreme, want nothing to do with these 'difficult' students, and those who, at the other extreme, become champions for these neglected students and take their side against their colleagues.

An example of this was in a comprehensive school, where a behaviour support specialist was recruited to the senior management team. He immediately came into conflict with fellow senior managers about what he saw as their over-emphasis on the national curriculum and public examination results. Rather than trying to work with his colleagues in a co-operative manner, and try to move their thinking gradually towards his, he slated them and accused them of being uncaring about the needs of students at risk of exclusion, and ignorant of how to support them. Not only were his colleagues insulted by this behaviour, they thought that it revealed ignorance and naivety about the national educational policy. As a result he became marginalised by the management team who went on to make disastrous decisions leading to an increase in disruptive and anti-social behaviour in the school. Programmes which the behaviour specialist worked on with at-risk students failed because of a lack of whole school support.

In schools where such polarisation is rife, staff as well as students can become marginalised and excluded. Worse still, staff and students may form unhealthy alliances and subtly condone disruptive behaviour. This situation is clearly no help to the school, the staff, or the students involved.

There is no simple resolution to the dilemmas posed by these kinds of conflicts. The crucial thing here is that staff learn to support each other in working towards a set of common goals that apply to all students. This point is supported by a DFEE-sponsored study (Daniels, Visser, Cole and de Reykebill, 1999) of thirty mainstream schools (thirteen primary) deemed by Ofsted to be offering effective provision for children with EBDs. It identified five common features associated with good practice:

- *Leadership*: heads and SMTs provided effective leadership, particularly in communicating appropriate values, ethos and aspirations for the school as a whole.

- *Sharing Values*: a core of staff working co-operatively with one another and pupils to ensure the active participation of all students, and who critically reflect on and learn from their own actions.

- *Behaviour Policy and Practice*: A common behaviour policy for all pupils and staff. A consistent, well-monitored behaviour policy in which there is consistency between approaches to dealing with pupils with EBD and those who do not have EBD.

- *Understanding EBD*: key members of staff who understand the nature of emotional and behavioural difficulties, and are able to distinguish these from routine misbehaviour.

- *Teaching Skills and the Curriculum*: necessity of including opportunities for children to learn from their own actions, through active involvement in learning tasks and the need for an appropriately challenging curriculum. This is important for all pupils.

In effective schools staff support one another both professionally and personally (Cooper *et al.*, 2000). They talk openly about difficulties they experience in their classrooms and treat these not as admissions of failure but as problems to be solved by the whole school community. The emphasis in such schools is on shared ownership of problems, and a shared vested interest in the success of all students and staff (see Chapter 7).

AD/HD and Family Life

If life in the school is difficult then life in the home situation is often worse. The families of children with AD/HD are often subject to a wide range of stressors (Everett and Everett, 1999). The marriages of parents of children with AD/HD can be severely affected, with parents suffering feelings of grief, shame and fear as a result of their child being diagnosed. Sometimes these feelings can manifest themselves in the form of arguments and recriminations in which parents blame each other for the child's condition, or argue about approaches to management.

A major characteristic of AD/HD is the tendency of children with the condition to be unresponsive to parental management strategies. This can cause chaos inside and outside the home and lead to a loss of parental confidence in their ability to 'handle' their children. This problem can be exacerbated by the uninformed judgements of neighbours, 'friends', relatives and complete strangers, who jump to the conclusion that the child's problems are the parents' fault. In some cases long-standing friendships are broken off, and grandparents come into conflict with the parents, and sometimes openly reject the child with AD/HD.

While all this is going on the child with AD/HD's need for a calm, predictable and secure environment is likely to be undermined, with the possible consequence of additional difficulties being created, such as oppositionality or defiant behaviour.

Where there are siblings, fallout from this family mayhem may involve brothers or sisters being ignored or neglected, sometimes leading to resentment and emotional problems. At other times, well-behaved siblings may be held up in comparison to the child with AD/HD, leaving the child with AD/HD feeling hurt and rejected. It can be particularly humiliating to the child with AD/HD to be compared unfavourably to a sibling who is younger but more competent than the older child in social, behavioural and/or educational matters.

Whilst these kinds of problems do not in themselves cause AD/HD they certainly make it worse for the affected child. They also put the stability of the family unit at risk.

Schools cannot be expected to take responsibility for resolving family difficulties, but they can make a contribution by:

- Being welcoming and supportive to parents, and acting as a source of information about the nature of the child's difficulties and ways of dealing with them. In particular it is important that parents feel that there is a person at the school who will give them a sympathetic ear when they need it.

- Helping to put parents in touch with other parents experiencing difficulties with children in the same school.

- Having available details of local and national support groups for parents of children with AD/HD and related problems.

- Making school premises available for meetings of local support groups, and engaging in joint activities with them, such as fund-raising, providing public information days, etc.

- Having relevant literature on display, such as leaflets from charitable and other organisations.

- Displaying details of family support services, such as child and family guidance centres, social services, along with details of referral procedures.

A Word About Dads

Both of the authors of this book have engaged over the years in many training events relating to AD/HD and similar problems. One thing that we have noticed is the overwhelming preponderance of women in audiences for these events. This has been true in such diverse locations as England, Scotland, Ireland, Germany, the USA, Japan, Korea and Taiwan. We have puzzled about this for some time, and have come up with a variety of explanations:

- There are more women than men in the professions most likely to come into close contact with children with AD/HD (such as teaching, child care, nursing).

- The division of labour is such that women are still more likely than men to take the lead in child care arrangements in the home.

- Males are far more likely to have AD/HD than females, especially if they are the parent of a child with AD/HD. Women attend in part, therefore, out of curiosity about the enigma of maleness. Men would like to attend, but are too inattentive to sit through a lecture, or too disorganised to find out when and where the venue is, or, having decided to go to the lecture, at the last minute they do something else on an impulse.

- Men have heard that some lecturers make facetious jokes about AD/HD among adult males, and are put off attending because of this.

Whatever the reason, or reasons, for the absence of males at these events, there are good reasons why they should be as involved as their female partners in dealing with their children's AD/HD. This is because the more adults in a child's life who have an informed understanding of his or her difficulties the better. Children and young people with AD/HD thrive when the adults around them present a united front and take an informed and consistent approach to their management.

More specifically, there may be a particular place in the management of AD/HD for positive male role models. This is because the symptoms of AD/HD can be seen as the extreme embodiment of certain male stereotypes which are promoted by certain forms of popular media. Both dramatic and comic TV programmes present male characters who are impulsive, restless, and rebellious in an attractive light. These characters are often contrasted with strong, self-possessed female characters. A good example of this is the BBC programme *Men Behaving Badly*. Popular soap operas such as *East Enders* and *Brookside* have similar characters. The internationally popular animated series, *The Simpsons*, reflects a similar pattern, with one of its key characters, the mischievous Bart, actually being diagnosed with AD/HD in one episode. Although the comic characters are often portrayed in an ironic light this does not detract from their magnetic charm on which the popularity of these programmes depends. The extent to which these TV shows influence children's behaviour is debatable. This is not the point. What is being suggested is that programmes reflect and reinforce the popular image of the 'lovable rogue' which is embedded in our culture. This makes the need for positive models of men able to exert control over their impulses necessary.

A Consistent and Human Approach

We have talked a great deal in this book about behaviour expectations, and techniques that can be used to influence the student's behaviour. These approaches are vital in helping students develop the internal controls necessary for positive social and educational progress. Finally, we would like to emphasise the importance of the human touch. We suggest that the interaction and intervention with the child with AD/HD should always be carried out in a way that retains a sense of proportion and humanity. With this in mind we would like to leave the reader with a list of cautions that could usefully apply to interactions between all adults and children, and especially parents/teachers and children with AD/HD.

1. Ask *what really matters*

For example, is it more important for the child to arrive at school calm and cheerful rather than being forced to tidy the room before leaving the house? It is probably more important to start the day in a calm and harmonious way. This will give him or her a positive frame of mind, and maximise the chance that when he/she comes home in the afternoon he/she will be willing to carry out the dreaded tidying chore.

2. Keep an open mind

Not everything a child with AD/HD does should be interpreted in terms of AD/HD. There is no such thing as an AD/HD child; there are children, however, with AD/HD for whom AD/HD is only a part of their make-up.

3. Be flexible

Be prepared to admit you could be in the wrong and change your strategy if it is not working.

4. Be Responsive

Give the child frequent and consistent feedback and consequences.

5. Be positive

Try to use rewards rather than punishments. Rewarding good behaviour is not a form of bribery. Rewards are earned and given when they are deserved.

6. Be honest

The child should be told when his or her behaviour is unacceptable, but it should be clear that it is the behaviour and not the child that is unacceptable. Practise forgiveness.

7. Take care of yourself

Acknowledge your feelings and know your limits. Being exhausted and angry are human responses to stressful situations. When these feelings arise they are a signal that you need to step back and relax, even if it is only for a moment or two.

8. Keep a sense of proportion

Finally one of the most powerful human attributes is a sense of humour. Keep things in perspective, do your best, and remember life is too short not to enjoy it.

As H. Jackson Brown put it: 'Success is getting what you want, Happiness is liking what you get.'

Appendix 1

DSM IV Diagnostic Criteria for Attention-Deficit/Hyperactivity Disorder

A. Either (1) or (2):

1. six (or more) of the following symptoms of *inattention* have persisted for at least 6 months to a degree that is maladaptive and inconsistent with developmental level:

Inattention
  (a) often fails to give close attention to details or makes careless mistakes in schoolwork, work, or other activities;
  (b) often has difficulty sustaining attention in tasks or play activities;
  (c) often does not seem to listen when spoken to directly;
  (d) often does not follow through on instructions and fails to finish schoolwork, chores, or duties in the workplace (not due to oppositional behaviour or failure to understand instructions);
  (e) often has difficulty organising tasks and activities;
  (f) often avoids, dislikes, or is reluctant to engage in tasks that require sustained mental effort (such as schoolwork or homework);
  (g) often loses things necessary for tasks or activities (e.g. toys, school assignments, pencils, books, or tools);
  (h) is often easily distracted by extraneous stimuli;
  (i) is often forgetful in daily activities.

2. six (or more) of the following symptoms of *hyperactivity-impulsivity* have persisted for at least 6 months to a degree that is maladaptive and inconsistent with developmental level:

Printed here with kind permission of the American Psychiatric Association from: Diagnostic and Statistical Manual of Mental Disorders, 4th edn (Washington, DC: APA, 1994).

Hyperactivity
(a) often fidgets with hands or feet or squirms in seat;
(b) often leaves seat in classroom or in other situations in which remaining seated is expected;
(c) often runs about or climbs excessively in situations in which it is inappropriate (in adolescents or adults, may be limited to subjective feelings of restlessness);
(d) often has difficulty playing or engaging in leisure activities quietly;
(e) is often 'on the go' or often acts as if 'driven by a motor';
(f) often talks excessively.

Impulsivity
(g) often blurts out answers before questions have been completed;
(h) often has difficulty awaiting turn;
(i) often interrupts or intrudes on others (e.g. butts into conversation or games).

B. Some hyperactive-impulsive or inattentive symptoms that caused impairment were present before age 7 years.

C. Some impairment from the symptoms is present in two or more settings (e.g. at school [or work] and at home).

D. There must be clear evidence of clinically significant impairment in social, academic, or occupational functioning.

E. The symptoms do not occur exclusively during the course of a Pervasive Developmental Disorder, Schizophrenia, or other Psychotic Disorder and are not better accounted for by another mental disorder (e.g. Mood Disorder, Anxiety Disorder, Dissociative Disorder, or a Personality Disorder).

Code based on type:
314.01 *Attention-Deficit/Hyperactivity Disorder, Combined Type*:
        if both Criteria A1 and A2 are met for the past 6 months.

314.0   *Attention-Deficit/Hyperactivity Disorder, Predominantly Inattentive Type*:
        if Criterion A1 is met but Criterion A2 is not met for the past 6 months.

314.02 *Attention-Deficit/Hyperactivity Disorder, Predominantly Hyperactive-Impulsive Type*:
        if Criterion A2 is met but Criterion A1 is not met for the past 6 months.

Coding note: For individuals (especially adolescents and adults) who currently have symptoms that no longer meet full criteria, 'In Partial Remission' should be specified.

Appendix 2

ICD10   F90 Hyperkinetic Disorder

Note: The research diagnosis of hyperkinetic disorder requires the definite presence of abnormal levels of inattention, hyperactivity, and restlessness that are pervasive across situations and persistent over time and that are not caused by other disorders such as autism or affective disorders.

G1.   *Inattention*. At least six of the following symptoms of inattention have persisted for at least 6 months, to a degree that is maladaptive and inconsistent with the developmental level of the child:

   (1)   often fails to give close attention to details, or makes careless errors in schoolwork, work, or other activities;
   (2)   often fails to sustain attention in tasks or play activities;
   (3)   often appears not to listen to what is being said to him or her;
   (4)   often fails to follow through on instructions or to finish schoolwork, chores, or duties in the workplace (not because of oppositional behaviour or failure to understand instructions);
   (5)   is often impaired in organising tasks and activities;
   (6)   often avoids or strongly dislikes tasks, such as homework that requires sustained mental effort;
   (7)   often loses things necessary for certain tasks or activities, such as school assignments, pencils, books, toys or tools;
   (8)   is often easily distracted by external stimuli;
   (9)   is often forgetful in the course of daily activities.

Printed here with kind permission of The World Health Organization from: WHO, *The International Classification of Diseases*, 10th edn (Vienna: WHO, 1990).

G2. *Hyperactivity*. At least three of the following symptoms of hyperactivity have persisted for at least 6 months, to a degree that is maladaptive and inconsistent with the developmental level of the child:

> (1) often fidgets with hands or feet or squirms on seat;
> (2) leaves seat in classroom or in other situations in which remaining seated is expected;
> (3) often runs about or climbs excessively in situations in which it is inappropriate (in adolescents or adults, only feelings of restlessness may be present);
> (4) is often unduly noisy in playing or has difficulty in engaging quietly in leisure activities;
> (5) exhibits a persistent pattern of excessive motor activity that is not substantially modified by social context or demands.

G3. *Impulsivity*. At least one of the following symptoms of impulsivity has persisted for at least 6 months, to a degree that is maladaptive and inconsistent with the developmental level of the child:

> (1) often blurts out answers before questions have been completed;
> (2) often fails to wait in lines or await turns in games or group situations;
> (3) often interrupts or intrudes on others (e.g. butts into others' conversations or games);
> (4) often talks excessively without appropriate response to social constraints.

G4. Onset of the disorder is not later than the age of 7 years.

G5. *Pervasiveness*. The criteria should be met for more than a single situation, e.g. the combination of inattention and hyperactivity should be present both at home and at school, or at both school and another setting where children are observed, such as a clinic. (Evidence for cross-situationality will ordinarily require information from more than one source; parental reports about classroom behaviour, for instance, are unlikely to be sufficient.)

G6. The symptoms in G-G3 cause clinically significant distress or impairment in social, academic, or occupational functioning.

G7. The disorder does not meet the criteria for pervasive developmental disorders (F84–), manic episode (F30–), depressive episode (F32–), or anxiety disorders (F41–).

Comment
Many authorities also recognise conditions that are sub-threshold for hyperkinetic disorder. Children who meet criteria in other ways but do not show abnormalities of hyperactivity/impulsiveness may be recognised as showing *attention deficit*; conversely, children who fall short of criteria for attention problems but meet criteria in other respects may be recognised as showing *activity disorder*. In the same way, children who meet criteria for only one situation (e.g. only the home or only the classroom) may be regarded as showing a *home-specific* or *classroom-specific disorder*. These conditions are not yet included in the main classification because of

insufficient empirical predictive validation, and because many children with sub-threshold disorders show other syndromes (such as oppositional defiant disorder, F91.3) and should be classified in the appropriate category.

F90.0   *Disturbance of activity and attention*
        The general criteria for hyperkinetic disorder (F90) must be met, but not those for conduct disorders (F91–).

F90.1   *Hyperkinetic conduct disorder*
        The general criteria for both hyperkinetic disorder (F90) and conduct disorders (F91–) must be met.

F90.8   *Other hyperkinetic disorders*

F90.9   *Hyperkinetic disorder, unspecified*
        This residual category is not recommended and should be used only when there is a lack of differentiation between F90.0 and F90.1 but the overall criteria for F90– are fulfilled.

A Note on the Relationship Between the DSM-IV and ICD-10 Criteria

Although there are very close similarities between the two diagnostic criteria, there are significant differences also. The main differences relate to the roles of impulsivity and hyperactivity in the different criteria. In the DSM hyperactivity and impulsivity are bracketed together whilst they are separate in the ICD 10 criteria. This means that children can receive the DSM diagnosis without displaying any symptoms of 'impulsivity'. Furthermore, the items relating to noisy play and excessive talking are more restricted in the ICD 10 than the DSM. These differences result in fewer but more severely affected children being identified by the ICD 10 than the DSM, leading clinicians to conclude that the ICD diagnosis is best seen as sub-part of the more inclusive DSM diagnosis (Munden and Arcelus, 1999; Overmeyer and Taylor, 1999; Barkley, 1990).

References

American Psychiatric Association (1994) *Diagnostic and Statistical Manual of Mental Disorders*, Washington: APA.

Baddeley, J. (1986) *Working Memory*, Oxford: Clarendon Press.

Barkley, R. (1990) *AD/HD: A Handbook for Diagnosis and Treatment*, New York: Guilford.

—— (1997) *ADHD and the Nature of Self Control*, New York: Guilford.

Blau, B. (1996) 'Oppositional defiant disorder', in G. Blau and T. Gullotta (eds), *Adolescent Dysfunctional Behavior*, Thousand Oaks, CA, London and New Delhi: Sage.

Borger, N. and Van der Meere, J. (2000) 'Visual behaviour of ADHD children during an attention test', *Journal of Child Psychology and Psychiatry*, 41(4), 525–32.

BPS (British Psychological Society) (2000) *AD/HD: Guidelines and Principles for Successful Multi-Agency Working*, Leicester: BPS.

Bruner, J. (1987) 'The transactional self', in J. Bruner and H. Haste (eds), *Making Sense*, London: Cassell.

—— and Haste, H. (eds) (1987) *Making Sense*, London: Cassell.

Cooper, P. (1993) *Effective Schools for Disaffected Students*, London: Routledge.

—— and Bilton, K. (1999) *AD/HD: Research, Practice and Opinion*, London: Whurr.

—— Drummond, M., Hart, S., Lovey, J. and McLaughlin, C. (2000) *Positive Alternative to Exclusion*, London: Routledge.

—— and Ideus, K. (1996) *AD/HD: A Practical Guide For Teachers*, London: Fulton.

—— and McIntyre, D. (1996) *Effective Teaching and Learning: Teachers' and Students' Perspectives*, Buckingham, Open University.

—— and Shea, T. (1999) 'AD/HD from the inside: an empirical study of young people's perceptions of AD/HD', in P. Cooper and K. Bilton (eds), *AD/HD: Research, Practice and Opinion*, London: Whurr.

—— and Upton, G. (1990) 'An ecosystemic approach to emotional and behavioural difficulties in schools', *Educational Psychology*, 10(4), 301–21.

—— Smith, C. J. and Upton, G. (1994) *Emotional and Behavioural Difficulties: Theory to Practice*, London: Routledge.

Crammond, B. (1994) 'AD/HD and creativity: two sides of the same coin?' Paper presented at the Annual Meeting of the American Educational Research Association, New Orleans.

Daniels, H., Visser, J., Cole, T. and de Reykebill, N. (1999) *EBD in Mainstream Schools*, London: DFEE.

Detweiller, R., Hicks, A. and Hicks, M. (1999) 'A multimodal approach to the assessment and management of AD/HD', in P. Cooper and K. Bilton (eds), *AD/HD: Research, Practice and Opinion*, London: Whurr.

DuPaul, G. and Stoner, G. (1994) *AD/HD in the Schools: Assessment and Intervention Strategies*, New York: Guilford.

Everett, C. and Everett, S. (1999) *Family Therapy for AD/HD*, New York: Guilford.

Farrington, D. (1990) 'Implications of criminal career research for the prevention of offending', *The Journal of Adolescence*, 13, 93–113.

Frith, U. (1992) 'Cognitive development and cognitive deficit', *The Psychologist*, 5, 13–19.

Goldstein, S. (1995) *Understanding and Managing Children's Classroom Behavior*, Chichester: Wiley.

Goodman, R. (1997) 'The strengths and difficulties questionnaire: a research note', *Journal of Child Psychology and Psychiatry*, 38, 581–5.

—— (1999) 'The extended version of the strengths and difficulties questionnaire as a guide to child psychiatric caseness and consequent burden', *Journal of Child Psychology and Psychiatry*, 40(5), 791–800.

Graham, P. (1991) *Child Psychiatry: A Developmental Approach*, Oxford: Oxford University Press.

Greenhill, L. (1998) 'Childhood ADHD: pharmacological treatments', in P. Nathan and M. Gorman (eds), *A Guide to Treatments that Work*, Oxford: Oxford University Press.

Hallowell, E. and Ratey, J. (1995) *Driven to Distraction*, London: Touchstone Books.

Harizuka, S. (1998) 'Historical overview and prospects for the practical use of psychological rehabilitation (Dohsa Hou)', *Research Bulletin of Educational Psychology*, Faculty of Education, Kyushu University, 43(1), 63–70.

Hartmann, T. (1993) *ADD: A Different Perception*, Novato, CA: Underwood-Miller.

Hayden, C. (1997) 'Exclusion from primary school: children in need and children with special educational need', *Emotional and Behavioural Difficulties*, 2(3), 36–44.

Henggeler, S. (1999) 'Multisystemic therapy: an overview of clinical procedures, outcomes and policy implications', *Child Psycholgy and Psychiatry Review*, 4(1), 2–10.

Hill, P. and Cameron, M. (1999) 'Recognising hyperactivity: a guide for the cautious clinician', *Child Psychology and Psychiatry Review*, 4(2), 50–60.

Hinshaw, S. (1994) *Attention Deficits and Hyperactivity in Children*, London, New York, New Delhi: Sage.

—— Klein, R. and Abikoff, H. (1998) 'Childhood ADHD: non-pharmacological and combination treatments', in Nathan and M. Gorman (eds), *A Guide to Treatment That Works*, Oxford: Oxford University Press.

Jordan, D. (1992) *Attention Deficit Disorder*, Austin, TX: Pro-Ed.

Kewley, G. (1999) *AD/HD: Recognition, Reality and Resolution*, Horsham: LAC Press.

Kinder, J. (1999) 'ADHD a different viewpoint: holistic and other approaches', in P. Cooper and K. Bilton (eds), *ADHD: Research, Practice and Opinion*, London: Whurr.

Kolb, D. (1984) *Experience and Learning*, Englewood Cliffs, NJ: Prentice-Hall.

Laslett, R. and Smith, C. J. (1995) *Effective Classroom Management*, 2nd edn, London, Routledge.

Layzell, P. (1995) 'Case study of a school–parent liaison programme,' *Therapeutic Care and Education*, 4(2): 23–31.

McArdle, P., O'Brien, G. and Colvin, I. (1995) 'Hyperactivity, Prevalence and relation with conduct disorder', *Journal of Child Psychology and Psychiatry*, 36, 279–303.

Meighan, R. (2000) 'Home based education: not "does it work?" but "why does it work?"' *Topic*, 23, Spring, 1–9.

Mills, H. (1996) 'Anxiety disorders,' in G. Blau and T. Gullotta (eds), *Adolescent Dysfunctional Behavior*, Thousand Oaks, CA, London and New Delhi: Sage.

Molnar, A. and Lindquist, B. (1989) *Changing Problem Behavior*, San Francisco: Jossey Bass.

Munden, A. and Arcelus, J. (1999) *The AD/HD Handbook*, London: Jessica Kingsley.

Naruse, G. (1975) 'The psychological treatment of motor difficulties in cerebral palsied children', *Journal of Rehabilitation Psychology*, 3, 1–10.

NICE (National Institute of Clinical Excellence) (2000) *Guidance on the Use of Methylphenidate for AD/HD*, London: NICE.

Nigg, J. and Hinshaw, S. (1998) 'Parent personality traits and psycho pathology associated with antisocial behaviors in childhood ADHD', *Journal of Child Psychology and Psychiatry*, 39(2), 145–59.

Olsen, J. (1997) *Managing Classroom Gambits*, Canberra: Author.

Overmeyer, S. and Taylor, E. (1999) 'Principles of treatment for hyperkinetic disorder: practice approaches for the UK', *Journal of Child Psychology and Psychiatry*, 40(8), 1147–57.

Pellegrini, A. and Horvat, M. (1995) 'A developmental and contextualist critique of AD/HD', *Educational Researcher*, 24 (1), 13–20.

—— Huberty, P. and Jones, I. (1996) 'The effects of recess timing on children's playground and classroom behaviors', *American Educational Research Journal*, 32(4), 845–64.

Place, M., Wilson, J., Martin, E. and Hulsmeir, J. (2000) 'The frequency of emotional and behavioural disturbance in an EBD school', *Child Psychology and Psychiatry Review*, 5(2), 76–80.

Pliszka, S., Carlson, C. and Swanson, J. (1999) *AD/HD With Comorbid Disorders: Clinical Assessment and Management*, New York: Guilford.

Sergeant, J. (1995) 'Hyperkinetic disorder revisited', in J. Sergeant (ed.), *Eunythydis: European Approaches to Hyperkinetic Disorder*, Amsterdam: Sergeant.

Still, G. (1902) 'Some abnormal psychical conditions in children', *The Lancet*, 1, 1008–12, 1077–82, 1163–8.

Sullivan, K. (2000) 'School bullying: issues for teachers', *Topic*, 23, Spring, 1–7.

Tannock, R. (1998) 'ADHD: advances in cognitive, neurobiological and genetic research', *Journal of Child Psychology and Psychiatry*, 39 (1), 65–99.

Taylor, E. (1994) 'Hyperactivity as a special educational need', *Therapeutic Care and Education*, 4(2): 130–44.

Taylor, J. (1994) *Hyperactive/Attention Deficit Child*, Austen, TX: Pro-Ed.

Thompson, R. (1993) *The Brain: A Neuroscience Primer*, 2nd edn, New York: Freeman.

Walker, H., Colvin, G. and Ramsey, E. (1995) *Antisocial Behavior in School*, Pacific Grove, CA: Brooks/Cole.

Wallace, B. and Crawford, S. (1994) 'Instructional paradigms and the AD/HD child', in C. Weaver (ed.), *Success at Last: Helping Students with AD(H)D Achieve their Potential*, Portsmouth, NH: Heinemann.

Weaver, C. (ed.) (1994) *Success at Last: Helping Students with AD(H)D Achieve their Potential*, Portsmouth, NH: Heinemann.

Webster-Stratton, C. (1999) *How to Promote Children's Social and Emotional Competence*, London: Paul Chapman.

Wheldall, K. and Merrett, F. (1987) 'Training teachers to use the behavioural approach to classroom management', in K. Wheldall (ed.), *The Behaviourist in the Classroom*, London: Allen and Unwin.

Van der Meere, J. (1996) 'The role of attention', in S. Sandberg (ed.), *Monographs in Child and Adolescent Psychiatry: Hyperactivity Disorders of Childhood*, Cambridge: Cambridge University Press.

Vygotsky, L. (1987) *Collected Works*, London: Pellum.

World Health Organisation (1990) *International Classification of Diseases*, 10th edn, Geneva: WHO.

Young Minds (1999) 'Fact Sheet No. 1', London: Author.

Index